FRAUD 101

FRAUD 101

Techniques and Strategies for Detection

Second Edition

Howard Silverstone
Howard R. Davia

WILEY

JOHN WILEY & SONS, INC.

Published by John Wiley & Sons, Inc., Hoboken, New Jersey
Published simultaneously in Canada

For general information on our other products and services, or technical support,
please contact our Customer Care Department within the United States at
800-762-2974, outside the United States at 317-572-3993 or fax 317-572-4002.

Wiley also publishes its books in a variety of electronic formats. Some content that
appears in print may not be available in electronic books.

For more information about Wiley products, visit our web site at www.wiley.com.

Library of Congress Cataloging-in-Publication Data:
Silverstone, Howard.
  Fraud 101 : techniques and strategies for detection / Howard Silverstone,
Howard R. Davia.—2nd ed.
    p. cm.
  Includes index.
  ISBN-13 978-0-471-72112-3
  ISBN-10 0-471-72112-3 (cloth)
  1. Commercial crimes—United States—Prevention. 2. Fraud investigation—
United States. I. Title: Fraud one hundred one. II. Davia, Howard R., 1947–
III. Title.
  HV6769.S55 2005
  363.25'963—dc22

                                                        2004025810

Printed in the United States of America

10 9 8 7 6 5 4 3 2 1

*This book is dedicated to my family
for supporting me in everything I do,
and to the memory of Howard Davia—
we never met, but we would have
so much to talk about.*

ACKNOWLEDGMENTS

I would like to thank my long-time friends and colleagues for their support and for their assistance with this book—particularly Kip Hamilton, CPA (Chapter 8), Jim Stavros, CPA (Appendix A), Chris Welde, CPA (Chapter 11) and Pat Woytek, CPA (Chapter 9).

Extra special thanks to my wife, Debbie, and to my children, Jonathan, Alec, and Emma for their never-ending love and support. Thanks also to my brother Phill and my parents Coba and Nat for continually raising my bar.

PREFACE

This book has been written to serve as a primer in proactive fraud-specific investigations. The events of recent years, including those involving Enron, WorldCom, and others, together with the Sarbanes-Oxley legislation and other corporate governance issues, have put fraud and especially corporate fraud securely on society's map. Society is still (and will always be) in need of the services of proactive fraud-specific investigations and investigators. The book has been written to provide basic instruction for everyone from college students to internal auditors with no training or experience in this craft, through the intermediate level of fraud investigator. Beyond that point the best instruction is interactive training between experienced instructors and investigators with at least intermediate skills.

The need for this book is summarized by the very nature of fraud, and specifically occupational fraud, as outlined by the Association of Certified Fraud Examiners in the *2004 Report to the Nation on Occupational Fraud and Abuse*:

> Occupational fraud schemes can be as simple as pilferage of company supplies or as complex as sophisticated financial statement frauds. All occupational fraud schemes have four key elements in common. The activity:
>
> - Is clandestine;
> - Violates the perpetrator's fiduciary duties to the victim organization;
> - Is committed for the purpose of direct or indirect financial benefit to the perpetrator; and
> - Costs the employing organization assets, revenue, or reserves.

Occupational fraud and abuse is a widespread problem that affects practically every organization, regardless of size, location, or industry. The ACFE has made it a goal to better educate the public and anti-fraud professionals about this threat.[1]

The book was originally written to provide the necessary background information needed for any reader—especially management readers—to fully appreciate the pernicious and largely uncontrolled nature of the fraud that threatens all entities today. The late Howard Davia set wonderful groundwork in his original version of this book. He urged independent auditors to take the necessary steps to begin to proactively perform auditing to discover fraud and provided the fundamental skills and methodology needed for all auditors to begin to perform fraud investigations. Finally, he attempted to cultivate an appropriate questioning attitude in the minds of prospective fraud examiners.

What I have done is to take Howard Davia's concepts and ideas and update them to reflect all the developments that have taken place in recent years. In the post-Enron, WorldCom, et al. world and living in the era of Sarbanes-Oxley and new auditing standards, it is important to update readers on the new tools for preventing and searching for fraud.

As a forensic accountant, I am conscious of the need for gathering evidence for public debate. To that end, and in the spirit of Howard Davia's original preface, this book and subsequent books on this subject will greatly benefit from the comments and recommendations of its readers. Accordingly, comments and recommendations are invited and will be carefully considered for inclusion in subsequent editions. These may be directed to hsilverstone@forensicresolutions.com.

NOTE

1. *2004 Report to the Nation on Occupational Fraud and Abuse*, Copyright by the Association of Certified Fraud Examiners.

CONTENTS

INTRODUCTION

Fraud was a very serious, underrated, and somewhat ignored threat to private and public entities for most of the nineteenth century. As a consequence, it prospered relatively undeterred and has cost many entities enormous sums of money (that they know of!). By the end of that century, however, there appeared to be a growing appreciation of the need to combat fraud more aggressively. However, effective combat was to be—and will continue to be for some time—elusive. It has always been human nature to wait until something happens until doing something about it, and the same holds true in business. Many business owners will not contemplate paying for proactive fraud services, but will end up spending a lot of money on lawyers and accountants after they discover their controller has stolen $600,000.

Business needs proactive fraud combatants now; however, there is still a shortage of trained proactive fraud examiners to respond to the need. Sarbanes-Oxley was passed in recognition of the fact that public companies need more accountability from the top. SAS 99 recognized that auditors need to be more skeptical of the occurrence of fraud. The American Institute of Certified Public Accountants (AICPA) continues to discuss the role of the auditor and working as part of a team with forensic accountants.

The concept of watching over one's books and records is nothing new. The father of double-entry bookkeeping, Luca Pacioli, is best known for his 1494 book *Summa de arithmetica, geometria, proportioni et proportionalita (The Collected Knowledge of Arithmetic, Geometry, Proportion and Proportionality)*. Within this book was a chapter entitled "Particularis de Computis et Scripturis," a treatise on accounting. It was this chapter that dealt with the principle of double-entry bookkeeping. He wrote of journals and ledgers, and he believed that a person should not go to sleep at night until the debits equaled the credits! His ideal ledger included assets (such as receivables and inventories), liabilities, capital, income, and expense accounts. Pacioli talked of year-end closing entries and suggested a trial balance be used to prove a balanced ledger. Also, his work refers to a wide range of topics from accounting ethics to cost accounting.

One of the most quoted lines from Pacioli's book, which bears so much relevance to our book, is as follows: "He who does business without knowing all about it, sees his money go like flies." Just like the accounting system Pacioli described over 500 years ago, this statement is as ageless and relevant today as it was half a millennium ago.[1]

Into the twentieth century society in general, and business specifically, was still seeing its money go like flies and did not have the capability to combat fraud. Whatever fraud investigation skills people possessed early in the nineteenth century had largely dissipated as a result of nonuse, and beginning any practice of proactive fraud-specific examinations was extremely difficult. Audit procedures for conducting proactive fraud-specific investigations are very different from those used to practice reactive fraud-specific examinations. In a proactive stance, the auditor has few if any clues that fraud has occurred. His or her job can literally be compared to hunting for a needle in a haystack. The proactive investigation has often been referred to as the watchdog, not the bloodhound. In reactive fraud-specific investigations, the professional begins with evidence that fraud has occurred (or has a good idea that it exists), knows what to look for, and perhaps where it may be found. His or her job is only to fully confirm and document it. Many auditors and/or investigators are skilled in reactive auditing. Very few are skilled in proactive fraud investigation.

This text provides fundamental training to undergraduate college students and practicing internal auditors and investigators up through the intermediate level. More advanced training is best suited to interactive settings—where more involved and realistic case studies can be discussed and studied—led by individuals experienced in fraud investigations. What makes this text unique is the fact that the original edition was written by an author who had considerable actual experience as a proactive fraud-specific auditor and upon whose personal experience much of this text is based. In addition, this updated version has been written and edited by someone with over 20 years of experience as a forensic accountant, and whose original training before that goes back to traditional accounting and auditing. This gives the added experience of hundreds of cases investigating suspected and known fraud, advising clients proactively to prevent fraud, and advising clients on financial transactions before they fall prey to fraudsters.

Of course, most perpetrators rarely discuss details of their crimes. As we will see in Chapter 1 and elsewhere in this book, external audits account for only 10 percent of initial fraud detection, with internal audits accounting for 24 percent. Together they account for over one-third of detected frauds—not bad, but not good enough—yet. Discovery through tips and by accident still account for almost two-thirds of known frauds. Perhaps the media attention devoted to recent corporate fraud and the subsequent legislation through Sarbanes-Oxley have increased public awareness. Hopefully, with the advent of hotlines and tip lines, the incidence of discovering fraud from tips will grow. On the other hand, proactive auditing standards such as SAS 99 may increase the number of frauds discovered by external audit.

Either way, and while it may seem a little perverse, this is an exciting time to be in the accounting and auditing profession, especially as a forensic accountant. It is as if the world has suddenly awakened to the things some of us have known for two decades and beyond—people steal and people cheat. Not computers. Not entities. People.

This text provides fundamental instruction to anyone interested in engaging in proactive fraud-specific investigations. It provides entry- to intermediate-level instruction for auditors who need to know what to search for, how to search for it, when they are finished, when the case in progress is ready for reactive case development, and when to quit. To assure complete understanding, it is enriched with illustrations and case studies selected to illuminate topics under discussion. All illustrations are either actual events or hypothetical examples structured from actual events from the authors' personal experiences. Many of the examples retained from the original text are timeless; they illustrate how fraud is nothing new and the methods in certain facets of business remain the same. Although this edition is augmented with many new examples, the true message intended by the original author remains in place.

NOTE

1. Excerpted from "Forensic Accounting and Fraud Investigations for Non-Experts," Howard Silverstone and Michael Sheetz, John Wiley & Sons, 2004.

1

THE WORLD OF FRAUD

Once or twice in my career I feel that I have done more real harm by my discovery of the criminal than ever he had done by his crime. I have learned caution now, and I had rather play tricks with the law of England than with my own conscience.[1]

Fraud presents us with a chicken and egg predicament. For all of the facts and war stories presented in this book, fraud is unavoidable, and for those in business, it is an occupational hazard. Our biggest challenge is to get it right—to ensure that business does not spend more money preventing and detecting fraud than it may possibly lose by it. Toward that end, when we receive a call or letter that someone is up to no good, we do not accuse the wrong person, or act on a tip that was given for the wrong reasons.

The cost of fraud and the long-term effects are many. Businesses that are victims of fraud not only bear the cost of the fraud itself (to the extent that they are unable to recover funds), but also the costs of investigating the fraud, of clearing up the problem, and of ensuring there is no recurrence.

Who steals my purse steals trash; 'tis something, nothing; 'twas mine, 'tis his, and has been slave to thousands; but he that filches from me my good name robs me of that which not enriches him and makes me poor indeed.[2]

As recent corporate incidents have shown us, financial losses arising from fraudulent activity may lead to layoffs, plant closures, or even business failures. For those companies able to survive a fraudulent event, they may still miss key business opportunities. The misappropriated capital might otherwise have been used to create employment, build new facilities, or develop better products and services. Fraud also extracts a huge personal cost. It can have a traumatic effect on individuals, leading, in some cases, to marriage breakups, nervous disorders, and even suicide.

We have to accept that no business and no one is immune to fraud. A business, agency, or individual that thinks it is invulnerable to fraud is, in fact, the most inviting to fraudsters. Too often complacency is the fraudster's best ally. Conversely, the fraudster's toughest foe is a potential target that turns out to be both vigilant and well prepared to meet this challenge. The bad news is that external audits no longer seem to be the deterrent they once were. In its *2002 Report to the Nation on Occupational Fraud and Abuse*, the Association of Certified Fraud Examiners (ACFE) reported that audited companies did suffer less severe fraud losses than unaudited ones. However, in its 2004 report, the ACFE noted that median losses are higher in organizations with an external audit, and it was "disappointing to find no trend indicating reduced losses as a result of external audits" (such a trend did exist in 2002).[3]

It is important to note that while fraud does not occur randomly throughout an organization, neither does it occur in statistical proportions. Of course, there are areas of any business that are more vulnerable than others and the work environment is the key factor affecting the occurrence of fraud. Fraud, by its very nature, usually means that the activities are not easily uncovered or identified. While external audit accounts for approximately 10 percent of initial fraud detection, it is encouraging to note that internal audit accounts for approximately 24 percent (up from approximately 19 percent in 2002). Elsewhere in this book we discuss Sarbanes-Oxley and other pronouncements but clearly, effective internal controls and internal audits have proven useful in the fight against fraud. Discovering fraud through tips and purely by accident combine to account for approximately 61 percent of initial detections, and are similar to the ACFE's report of 2002.

It is also important to remember that for all the case studies and war stories, for all the statistics and for all the discussion, we only know about the tip of the iceberg. Fraud is essentially broken into three primary groups: fraud that has been discovered and is detailed in the public domain; fraud that has been discovered, but the details have not been made public; and fraud that has not been detected.

For those of us who have been investigating and talking about fraud for so long, it is interesting to see that the concept of the anonymous letter (years ago referred to as the "poison pen letter"), whether from a loyal employee or vindictive ex-employee, is still an important key to the discovery of fraudulent activity. Through education and legislation, the implementation of tip lines and hotlines has furthered the progress of this means of initial detection. The ACFE still believes that companies need to do a better job of communicating the fact that they have a hotline, and need to reach out beyond the boundaries of their own organization to customers, vendors, and other third parties.

WHO COMMITS FRAUD AND WHY?

> *From a caprice of nature, not from the ignorance of man. Not a mistake has been made in the working. But we cannot prevent equilibrium from producing its effects. We may brave human laws, but we cannot resist natural ones.*[4]

Contrary to people's notion that computers stole their funds, fraud is carried out by people. While computers and other electronic wizardry may enable the deed, it is still the result of human input and motivation.

Therefore, a discussion about the human element is crucial to an understanding of fraud and will assist in the prevention and detection process. It is generally accepted within fraud prevention circles that a certain element of our society, and hence the population of any given organization, is inherently honest. Conversely, a certain element of people is inherently dishonest and little will deter them from deceit. The remaining element may commit acts of dishonesty if the need and opportunity coexist. Opinions vary on the percentages assigned to each element, with some believing the extremes range from 20 to 30 percent. This means that up to 80 percent of the workforce is potentially dishonest depending on the circumstances. The circumstances, of course, will be affected to the degree that there are adequate internal controls in place and that they are enforced.

As crime does not occur statistically, the honesty of employees in a company is not predetermined based on a statistical relationship. The business environment and culture will set the numbers. Thus, an honest person with a high degree of personal integrity may commit fraud given a set of situational pressures and high opportunity. Conversely, a person of low personal integrity may not commit fraud if he is not exposed to situational pressures and there are strong controls, which provide little or no opportunity for fraud.

Recent corporate events, and indeed the ensuing legislation, have recognized that management can control the situational pressures and the personal integrity of employees by not only knowing their people, but setting the tone themselves. Management can control the opportunities for fraud through internal controls, good management, good policies, and good procedures.

To illustrate this discussion further, let us imagine a person who is a pillar of their community, a well-respected, honest employee, a person with a background no more criminal than that of most of us. This person finds himself with an unshareable problem and an opportunity to steal money from his company. The chances are very good that if in that situation you walked up to him and said, "Fred, steal the money from your boss," he would look at you in horror as if you had suggested he could solve his problem by sticking a pistol into the face of the local liquor store owner. "Fred, steal the money from your company" probably would bring about less of a horror reaction. Still, honest and trusted persons just don't do those things. However, honest and trusted persons do "borrow," and if you were to suggest that Fred secretly borrow some money from his firm, you would have helped him over a tremendous hurdle. Then he would be able to tell himself that he is borrowing the money and he can continue to believe that he is an honest citizen, even as he is robbing the boss blind.

CASE 1.1 $3.28 Million Embezzled
Over 9 Years—Discovered When Savings Bank Alerted
Victim of Suspicious Transactions

A Maryland woman, on a salary of $36,000 a year, embezzled $3.28 million from a union general fund over a period of nine years before union officials became suspicious when a credit union notified union officials that large sums of money were moving in and out of union accounts. She had been responsible for transferring employee automatic payroll deductions to a credit union. She was required to issue one check to the credit union each pay period to cover all the employee deductions, to be credited to each employee's credit union account. Her scheme involved writing a larger check than was necessary and keeping the excess. She was able to cover the fraud by falsifying financial records and was also responsible for assuring that the accounts were in balance.[5]

FRAUD PREVENTION AND DETECTION

There is no special recipe, checklist, or manual on detecting fraud that can assist a business owner in his work. No such thing exists and no such thing is truly capable of being developed to address all forms of fraud. And therein, perhaps, lies a blessing. The development of material to assist the auditor in detecting fraud may create standards against which he or she may be held accountable. However, armed with a heightened awareness of the reality of fraud and the environmental factors and red flags that may signal the potential presence of fraudulent activities, accountants and businesses may be able to be more proactive in the prevention and detection of fraud.

However, what recent legislation has done is to instill in management the notion that they must:

- Accept that fraud exists and could occur.
- Acknowledge the importance of fraud awareness.
- Deal with the human factors by hiring honest people and keeping them honest via deterrents to fraud.
- Deal with the environmental factors by implementing adequate and enforced controls, policies, and procedures, including following up on all dishonest acts.

If you are a businessperson or work in the private sector or have clients in that position, protecting your or their bottom line from fraud is a challenging goal. But it can be achieved through the implementation of an effective prevention and detection strategy.

The elements of such a strategy include the need to:

- Understand why fraud is committed.
- Ensure that factors that may motivate employees to commit fraud are minimized.
- Understand the opportunities for fraud in the business.
- Pinpoint the exposures and high-risk areas and reduce the opportunities for fraud.

- Know the symptoms of fraud.
- Communicate expected behavior to employees.
- Respond appropriately to identified problems and seek out appropriate sanctions against the perpetrators.

CASE 1.2   The Protracted Payroll Fraud

Accidentally discovered, this case involved a woman who was employed by a university for 20 years. She embezzled $158,000 from the university over a period of seven years and no one at the university seemed to notice, despite the fact that during the seven years she was active, some of her thefts involved $149,190 in payroll checks written to ghost employees. The auditors certainly did not suspect her, and it is likely that they were never engaged in fraud-specific investigations. She was a highly respected employee of the university and was given the President's Award as the university's most valued employee.

Her luck changed, however, when postal service inspectors suspected her husband as being involved in a stolen check ring. While searching her residence for evidence of her husband's suspected crime, they found university payroll stubs under different names that she had saved. Their suspicions led to detection of her fraud. In a replay of the old story where the farmer locked the door to the barn after his horse was stolen, the university tightened payroll procedures.

In Chapter 2, we will discuss the role of the auditor in greater detail. However, it should be noted that historically internal auditors were perceived as not having enough training or experience to proactively detect fraud. Because many internal auditors came from independent auditors, and with little in accounting pronouncements until SAS 53, 82, and then 99, they brought no fraud investigation experience with them.

In addition, companies seemed reticent to spend a lot of resources, both physical and financial, for proactive investigations. While companies would spend money on fire insurance, hoping there would never be a fire, they questioned the value of fraud-specific examinations, because they had never had the problem in the past.

As a result of a combination of factors, the proactive and reactive landscape of fraud seems to have changed in the past couple of years. After the well-publicized scandals of WorldCom, Enron, and others, the era of Sarbanes-Oxley, greater corporate governance, and new auditing standards have all contributed to a more watchful eye and increased accountability.

As we noted earlier, you can never eliminate fraud, but you can reduce the possibility of it happening. The fact that initial detection of fraud by internal audit and internal controls has increased, as noted in the ACFE survey, points to increased awareness, accountability, and spending on such preventative methods.

NOTES

1. Sherlock Holmes in "The Adventure of Abbey Grange," Sir Arthur Conan Doyle.
2. *Othello*, William Shakespeare.
3. *2004 Report to the Nation on Occupational Fraud and Abuse*, Association of Certified Fraud Examiners.
4. Captain Nemo in *20,000 Leagues Under the Sea*, Jules Verne.
5. Todd Shields, "The Lifestyle Was too Good to be True." *Washington Post,* March 2, 1997, pp. B1, B4.

2

FRAUD COMBATANTS

Historically, there have been three types of combatants charged with the responsibility of keeping an eye on the financial well being of companies: the independent auditors, internal auditors, and criminal investigators. The independent auditors' job is a proactive one in that this auditor must determine the extent to which statements may need to be restated, but can be reactive if they actually find that a fraud has occurred. The role of the internal auditor has grown in the post-WorldCom and Enron world, together with the requirements under Sarbanes-Oxley for certification of financial statements, and is discussed elsewhere in this book.

The least proactive in terms of fraud detection have historically been the criminal investigators. They are typically retained once evidence of a fraud has been discovered, and are frequently hired to obtain corroborating evidence and compiling evidence necessary for prosecuting cases.

In the past couple of years, allegations of corporate fraud have dominated the headlines. These have included financial frauds at large companies, such as Enron and WorldCom, as well as high publicity matters such as Martha Stewart's stock scandal. The role of the outside investigator has now taken an interesting turn as the U.S. Securities and Exchange Commission has identified financial statement fraud as its "number one priority," while other federal criminal authorities have also committed to prosecute financial fraud.

FRAUD COMPANY PROFILE (1987–1997)

In a report commissioned by the Treadway Commission, entitled "Fraudulent Financial Reporting: 1987–1997, An Analysis of U.S. Public Companies,"[1] the Committee of Sponsoring Organizations of the Treadway Commission (COSO) analyzed the characteristics of approximately 200 financial statement fraud cases involving U.S. public companies to learn about the nature of the companies involved, the nature and size of the fraud, and the parties responsible for the fraud. One of the key findings of the COSO Report was that the companies committing financial statement fraud, at least during the period 1987 to 1997, were usually quite small, with revenues and assets generally under $50 million.

The COSO Report found that companies committing financial statement fraud often fit the following profile:

- They were small to mid-size, with less than $50 million in revenues or assets.
- They were often in a net loss or break-even position in the period prior to the beginning of the fraud.
- Concentrations were centered in the technology, healthcare, and financial services industries.
- The CEOs and CFOs were involved in the fraud.
- The founder/CFO appeared to dominate the organization.
- Boards and audit committees were very weak and owned a significant share of the company.
- The company manipulated revenues and/or assets; some frauds involved only disclosures.
- There were dire consequences for the company, often bankruptcy.

The New Profile (1997–2002)

As we all know from the headlines, times have changed. In the five-year period after the COSO Report, from 1997 to 2002, the size of reported restatements grew to unprecedented proportions. The companies restating have billions of dollars in revenues and assets, much larger than the prior profile of fraud in companies with less than $50 million in revenues and assets.

The nature of the industry in the profile has also changed. No longer do restatements tend to involve primarily technology, healthcare, and financial service companies. Today, financial statement fraud reaches across a wide variety of industries.

Another changed element in the profile involves the company's financial position prior to the restatement. These days, the companies restating were not operating at a net loss or break-even position at the time the fraud began. To the contrary, many of the companies were operating at a profit, and engaged in financial statement fraud to artificially maintain the appearance of continued growth.

AUDITOR RESPONSIBILITIES TO DETECT FRAUD

There's no business like show business, but there are several businesses like accounting.[2]

As noted earlier, we have seen a marked increase in the number of high profile companies under investigation for financial statement fraud and related accounting irregularities. However, one of the most frequently asked questions in the wake of these recent developments has been: "Where were the auditors when these irregularities occurred and why wasn't the fraud detected?"

There are three principal reasons why auditors may not detect fraud:

1. The first has to do with a general misunderstanding of the auditor's responsibilities in a financial statement audit, and misperceptions about the distinction between a financial statement audit and a fraud investigation.

2. The second is attributable to audit failure.

3. The third involves situations where the fraud was actively concealed from the auditors.

FINANCIAL STATEMENT AUDIT VERSUS FRAUD INVESTIGATION

There are five basic differences between a year-end financial statement audit and a fraud investigation. These differences relate to audit objective, scope, approach, standards, and training.

Objective

The objective of a financial statement audit is to obtain *reasonable assurance* about whether the financial statements are free from *material misstatement*, whether caused by error or fraud.

> *I have made the tough decisions, always with an eye toward the bottom line. Perhaps it's time America was run like a business.*[3]

The objective of a fraud investigation is to make an absolute determination about whether fraud exists, regardless of whether it is material or immaterial.

Scope

In order to obtain reasonable assurance that the financial statements are free from material misstatement, the scope of a financial statement audit is limited. A financial statement auditor typically reviews only a sample of selected transactions, on a test basis. If irregularities are detected, then the scope of the audit may be increased. In a fraud investigation, it is not uncommon to conduct a detailed review of every single transaction in those accounts where fraud is suspected.

Approach

In a financial statement audit, the auditor approaches the audit with an attitude of professional skepticism. This assumes that management is neither honest nor dishonest. In the accounting literature, professional skepticism is an attitude that includes a questioning mind and a critical assessment of audit evidence.

A fraud investigation is conducted with a higher degree of skepticism, with heightened scrutiny of all evidence and sources of information relating to questioned accounts.

Standards

Financial statement audits must be conducted in accordance with generally accepted accounting principles (GAAP) and in conformity with generally accepted auditing standards (GAAS). There are ten generally accepted auditing standards: three general standards, three standards of fieldwork, and four standards of reporting.

The three general standards require the audit to be conducted by persons with adequate technical training, independence in mental attitude, and due professional care in the performance of the audit.

The three standards of fieldwork require:

1. the work to be adequately planned and assistants properly supervised;
2. a sufficient understanding of internal controls to plan the audit tests; and
3. sufficient audit evidence to provide a reasonable basis for an opinion on the financial statements.

The four standards of reporting require the auditor's report to state:

1. whether the financial statements are presented in accordance with GAAP;
2. whether there are any instances in which accounting principles have not been consistently observed;
3. whether informative disclosures are reasonably accurate; and
4. the auditor's opinion on the financial statements or a statement that an opinion cannot be expressed.

Training

As a result of the four differences noted above, financial statement audits are conducted by independent auditors with technical audit training, while fraud investigations are generally conducted by forensic accountants with specialized training in fraud investigation and civil and criminal litigation.

FRAUD GUIDANCE

Statement on Auditing Standards (SAS) No. 99, "Consideration of Fraud in a Financial Statement Audit," was the first major audit standard issued after Sarbanes-Oxley. The AICPA stated that the new standard provides accountants with an excellent opportunity to repair some of the recent damage to the profession's reputation "one auditor, one engagement at a time."[4]

SAS 99 does not change the responsibility of the auditor as noted earlier, but hopes to improve the likelihood that an auditor will detect material misstatements in the financial statements caused by fraud. The audit team is required to set the tone for the audit by having a discussion of the importance of professional skepticism in planning the audit, and it reminds the auditor to have a questioning mind during the gathering and evaluation of audit evidence.

SAS 99 also provides for discussions among audit team members about the susceptibility of the financial statements to material misstatement due to fraud. The team members must be able to identify where the financial statements may be susceptible to fraud, how the company's management could conduct and conceal such a fraud, and how assets could be misappropriated by management or indeed by any employee.

As a fraud combatant the auditor, armed with the guidelines under SAS 99, should be more skeptical than ever. The AICPA believes that SAS 99 is "a comprehensive, far-reaching audit standard. It has the potential to significantly change the way we think about and perform audits."[5]

AUDIT DEFICIENCIES AND AUDIT FAILURES

As noted previously, the nature of a financial statement audit, unlike a fraud investigation, is not intended to provide absolute assurance against fraud. The auditors are merely required to seek out the presence of certain fraud risk factors. Historically, auditors were required to seek out the presence of certain fraud risk factors. This was typically done using a checklist approach, and had the inherent problem of failure to design the appropriate testing.

Of course, as we now know, intentional acts by corporate management to conceal the existence of fraud have been at the heart of many recently publicized cases.

The Top Ten Audit Deficiencies (1987–1997)

A complementary report by the authors of the COSO Report (entitled "Fraud Related SEC Enforcement Actions Against Auditors: 1987–1997"), documented the ten most common audit failures in

45 enforcement actions where the SEC imposed sanctions against auditors for their association with fraudulent financial statements during the period 1987 to 1997.

The top three deficiencies were:

1. The auditor's failure to gather sufficient audit evidence, including failure to corroborate management representations.
2. In about half of the enforcement actions reviewed, the auditors incorrectly applied or failed to apply GAAP pronouncements, as in Enron.
3. In 44 percent of the cases, audit program design was cited as a problem.

THE NEW WORLD

In a discussion memorandum "Forensic Services, Audits, and Corporate Governance: Bridging the Gap," the American Institute of Certified Public Accountants developed a paper to ". . . explore the ways in which forensic accounting professionals can provide assistance to audit committees, financial statement audit teams, and other corporate governance groups interested in the goal of improving financial reporting."[6]

While we do not intend to discuss the paper in full, it is interesting to see that a fraud combatant, the forensic accountant, is now portrayed in a watchdog/advisory position, in addition to what has historically been the bloodhound role—one who comes in when something is amiss. As a fraud combatant, the duties of the traditional auditor have been subjected to what is known as an expectation gap: the public thinks that auditors will find fraud, and should indeed attempt to seek out fraud at every turn of their audit. However, generally accepted auditing standards (GAAS) instruct the auditor to plan and perform an audit to obtain reasonable assurance that the statements are free of material misstatements, whether caused by error or fraud. The traditional auditors' role has essentially been that of watchdog, not bloodhound. Indeed in 1896, in the *Kingston Cotton Mills judgment in London, England*, the judge remarked that ". . . he is a watchdog but not a bloodhound. He is justified in believing tried servants of the company . . . entitled to assume that they are honest, and to rely upon their representations, provided he takes reasonable care."

The AICPA paper believes forensic accountants ". . . can play a vital role in combining investigative procedures with traditional audit procedures in a financial statement audit." The AICPA recognizes that forensic accountants have a different mind-set as they do not maintain the neutrality of traditional auditors, in other words, typically when a forensic accountant is brought into a situation, some event has already taken place.

What is most interesting about the AICPA's paper, and indeed the discussions subsequent to SAS 99, is that of the "fraud triangle"— where incentive and pressure, together with opportunity and rationalization or attitude, are present when fraud occurs. Those of us who have been in this field for some time have always discussed (as noted elsewhere in this book) the existence of the factors of need/greed, opportunity, and low expectation of being caught as the matches that start the fraud fire. Recognizing the fraud triangle is now an active combatant in the fight against fraud. By using auditing procedures to identify circumstances that create pressure or incentive is to understand the mind of the fraudster—not something that is historically taught to the young auditor.

The AICPA also notes that "an effective forensic accountant, operating in an audit environment, needs to have a sufficient understanding of the industry, as well as an understanding of accounting, auditing procedures, investigative techniques, evidence gathering, and the litigation process." These skill-sets represent a combination of both proactive and reactive investigations—a subject area covered in Chapters 4, 5, 10, and 11. Again, the skill-sets the AICPA recognizes in its paper are part-watchdog, part-bloodhound.

Continuing with our analogy, perhaps it is time our two dogs, the watchdog and the bloodhound, work together. First think of the traditional "junkyard" dog—the watchdog. Not much bite, but a lot of bark; trained to bark as soon as someone, anyone approaches the yard. Are they friend or foe? Is this a possible burglar? Through instinct, the watchdog barks upon sight or smell. However, not all those approaching are foes. There may be a legitimate reason this person is entering the yard after hours—perhaps the gate was still open for late deliveries, or perhaps this person has a key and is a new employee that the dog had not seen before.

Now, imagine the bloodhound sitting beside the watchdog. The bloodhound would be able to sense if the intruder was authorized to approach and whether the person used a key for entry or perhaps a password on an electronic gate. The bloodhound would also know there were security cameras covering the yard, monitored 24 hours a day by an outside, remotely located service, with a hotline to the local police upon sight of a possible unauthorized intruder. The bloodhound has been down this road before, normally brought in to sniff around for clues after the bad deed was done.

So, do the watchdog and bloodhound sit side-by-side in the yard?

The AICPA asks that question in its paper: ". . . a key variable that will need to be focused on is whether the forensic accountants will be acting as members of the audit team, or will be separately engaged by management or the audit committee." They also discuss whether they should be from the same firm or different firms. The outside issue obviously negates questions on independence, a subject of much discussion in the past couple of years, given the large corporate collapses.

Perhaps the strongest form of fraud combat recognized by the AICPA paper is enhancing professional skepticism and incorporating an "investigative mentality" in the audit. This requires more extensive corroboration of information and can include procedures such as the following, which were noted in the AICPA paper (and are typically done in a forensic investigation):

- Public Document Reviews and Background Investigations
- Analytical Procedures
- Brainstorming Session
- Interviews of Management and Others

At a recent seminar, the presenter used the analogy of the fox in the chicken coop. He likened the discussion with the fox to that of talking to management. Question: "Did you go in the chicken coop last night?" Response: "No!" Now, armed with analytics that show chickens are missing and after a brainstorming session, you interview others (i.e., the chickens). You can't interview all the chickens—that would be too time consuming, costly, and possibly duplicative. You look at the organization chart of the coop and decide to interview the supervising chicken and one of the line chickens. Question: "Do you believe someone other than a chicken was in the coop after hours last night?" Response: "Yes." Question: "Whom might that be?" Response: "The Fox!" An alternative question might be: "Was the fox in the coop last night?" Response: "You bet!" While no one may have seen the actual evidence to link the missing chickens with the fox, you do have incentive (personal gain by the fox), opportunity (a complete lack of security in the coop), and rationalization/attitude (nobody will miss a couple of chickens—the company can afford more).

This new combatant is summed up well, again by the AICPA in its discussion paper: "Forensic Accountants have emerged . . . as vital newly recognized allies in the fight against fraud." To the untrained eye, the problems of recent years are "new." As we discussed earlier, the expectation gap existed as long ago as 1896. Indeed, the major case of McKesson & Robbins in 1937 highlighted the need for better defined standards. Unfortunately, it is human nature to soon forget and slip once again into bad habits. However, with the combination of Sarbanes-Oxley, SAS 99, and continuing discussions as illustrated by the AICPA's paper, we seem to be fighting the battle on more fronts than we ever have in the past.

RECOMMENDED READING

1. Association of Certified Fraud Examiners, *2004 Report to the Nation on Occupational Fraud and Abuse*, 2004.
2. Discussion Memorandum, "Forensic Services, Audits and Corporate Governance: Bridging the Gap," American Institute of Certified Public Accountants, July 15, 2004.
3. *Fraudulent Financial Reporting: 1987–1997, An Analysis of U.S. Public Companies*, A research commissioned by the Committee of Sponsoring Organizations (COSO) of the Treadway Commission, November 30, 1999.
4. Howard Silverstone and Michael Sheetz, *Forensic Accounting and Fraud Investigation for Non-Experts*, Hoboken, NJ: John Wiley & Sons, 2004.
5. Tedd Avey, Ted Baskerville, Alan Brill, and the AICPA, *The CPA's Handbook of Fraud and Commercial Crime Prevention*, New York: American Institute of Certified Public Accountants, Inc., 2002.
6. G. Jack Bologna and Robert J. Lindquist, *Fraud Auditing and Forensic Accounting: New Tools and Techniques*, New York: John Wiley & Sons, 1995.
7. Albrecht and Albrecht, *Fraud Examination and Prevention*, Thompson Southwestern Publishing Company, 2004.
8. *The Numbers Game*, Speech presented to the New York University Center for Law and Business, September 28, 1998, www.sec.gov/news/speech/speecharchive/1998/spch220.txt.
9. Stephen Pizzo, Mary Fricker, and Paul Muolo, *Inside Job: The Looting of America's Savings and Loans*, New York: McGraw-Hill, 1989.
10. *The CPA's Role in Detecting and Preventing Fraud*, FBI Law Enforcement Bulletin 68, No. 7, July 1999.
11. *The Commission on Auditor's Responsibilities: Report, Conclusion and Recommendations*, New York: American Institute of Certified Public Accountants, 1978.

12. *Statement on Auditing Standard No. 99, Consideration of Fraud in a Financial Statement Audit*, New York: American Institute of Certified Public Accountants, 2002.

NOTES

1. The COSO Report, authored by Mark S. Beasley, Joseph V. Carcello, and Dana R. Hermanson, was published in 1999.
2. David Letterman, U.S. television host of the *Late Show with David Letterman*.
3. Donald Trump, entrepreneur; http://www.woopidoo.com/business_quotes /authors/donald-trump-quotes.htm.
4. AICPA Practice Aid Series, *Fraud Detection in a GAAS Audit: SAS 99 Implementation Guide*, 2003.
5. Ibid.
6. "Forensic Services, Audits, and Corporate Governance: Bridging the Gap," American Institute of Certified Public Accountants, July 15, 2004.

3

SARBANES-OXLEY AND ITS INFLUENCE ON FRAUD PREVENTION[1]

The Sarbanes-Oxley Act, passed in the wake of Enron and other scandals, seeks to reduce the likelihood of fraud by making public company CEOs and CFOs directly accountable for their organization's internal controls and financial disclosures. Senior managers will also be subject to greater oversight from more independent boards, internal audit committees, and external audits.

Rather than looking on the new law as imposing onerous requirements, management should view it as an opportunity to take a fresh look at the company's internal controls, to assess its risk of fraud, and to make changes where needed to reduce the organization's overall exposure to loss. The new emphasis on internal controls also offers corporate security the opportunity to become more involved in helping management prevent and detect fraud.

The goal of the new law is for internal controls to be so effective that degradation of the system through fraud is virtually impossible. While it can be argued that fraud can never be eliminated, the onus is on management to create the most effective system possible to prevent it and catch it. Audit firms will be asking very hard questions to see that this is so before certifying any management report, as their own review must withstand subsequent scrutiny by the SEC.

AUDIT COMMITTEE

What does a system of Sarbanes-Oxley-compliant controls look like? The first step toward compliance is the establishment of an audit committee. Every public company must have one. The members of the audit committee all have to be members of the board of directors but independent in the sense that they perform no other corporate duties and receive no compensation other than their directors' fees.

At least one member of the audit committee must be a financial expert. (The SEC will judge the level of expertise based on previous responsibilities, education, and experience with internal controls and the preparation of financial statements.) The audit committee is responsible for hiring and compensating both the auditors and any other consultants and is thus the logical body to oversee the entire compliance process from review through implementation.

Because audit committee members are drawn from the board of directors, a company may first need to revamp the board so that it can supply the financially experienced, independent members required by Sarbanes-Oxley. Although not spelled out by Sarbanes-Oxley, a significant control issue to be questioned by the external auditor will be the level of experience of the individuals on the board. Directors should be experienced businesspersons and as many as possible should be directors on other boards.

Another concern is whether board members have inappropriate ties to the company. A report, "Fraudulent Financial Reporting: 1987–1997, An Analysis of U.S. Public Companies," published in 1999 by the Committee of Sponsoring Organizations of the Treadway Commission (COSO), found that about 60 percent of the directors of fraudulent companies were insiders or so-called "gray" directors, that is, they had a high level of equity interest or some other personal or business connection with the company.

Sarbanes-Oxley states that audit committee members cannot be gray directors. Close family relationships among directors or the concentration of power in too few hands must also be questioned by external auditors. Sarbanes-Oxley is trying to make the charismatic CEO with a compliant board of inexperienced family members and cronies a thing of the past.

The audit committee must have the authority and resources to carry out its duties. As a rule, the committee should be active without being meddling. A written charter should set forth the meeting calendar, manner of reporting to the full board, audit plans, role of legal counsel, selection process for the external audit engagement, expense and compensation policy for the committee, and any other relevant matters. This charter should be developed with the assistance of management.

It may seem a simple and obvious matter, but the external auditor will certainly ask about the frequency of audit committee meetings. The 1999 COSO report found that the audit committees of fraudulent companies usually met only once a year. Once every quarter should be the minimum.

Because the separation of the audit and accounting firm consulting function is one of the key elements of Sarbanes-Oxley, the audit committee should be especially aware of all consulting engagements and make sure that there are no conflicts of interest. The committee should also act to ensure the total independence of the external auditors and review all consulting and external audit fees.

Committee members should be prepared to question management on any unusual transactions or novel practices. The committee should also discuss with the external auditor any questions the auditor discussed with management, and it should not be afraid to demand answers to any of the committee members' own questions.

The audit committee should be especially vigilant in exercising its oversight authority if, after a disagreement with the auditors, management seeks a second opinion or requests a change of auditor. Genuine differences of opinion among accounting experts do, indeed, occur. Sometimes, however, management may be seeking a favorable opinion to ensure its bonuses or it may wish to slip a fraudulent transaction past the auditors. Audit committee members must exercise the full force of their experience, impartiality, and knowledge in these difficult cases.

The chair of the audit committee should, as a matter of policy, keep an open door for the chief internal auditor, the security director, and the CFO and have good communications with the engagement partner of the external auditor. Since the Sarbanes legislation, many companies have set up hotlines that let their employees use various communication methods (such as voicemail) to report suspected incidents and hold confidential discussions with members of the audit committee. A receptive and cooperative attitude means early knowledge of trouble and reduces response time. Problems can never be allowed to fester because the chair of the audit committee was unapproachable.

CODE OF ETHICS

The next step should be the establishment of a code of ethics, which must apply equally to front-line employees and senior executives. Of course, a code of ethics is only as good as the willingness of employees to be governed by it; no code can stop a person determined to commit fraud. But criminologists have shown again and again that employees who commit fraud are not hardened criminals; rather, they are average people who, faced with either temptation or financial crisis, will turn to fraud if the opportunity arises.

Good internal controls can help to reduce the opportunity for crime (more on this later). But the corporate culture also plays a role. Employee attitudes are shaped to some extent by the attitudes of senior management. Where management is seen to be adhering to the highest standards of business practice, employees are more likely to do the same. Thus, the role of the code of ethics is to set the right tone and to dissuade good people from making wrong choices in their moments of weakness or crisis.

Sarbanes-Oxley recognizes this moral responsibility of senior management and the audit committee. Sarbanes-Oxley requires any code to focus on conflicts of professional and personal interest, full disclosure of relevant matters in the company's regular filings, and compliance with government rules and regulations. This section seems aimed at preventing a repetition of improper insider trading. The code of ethics should be written and thoroughly explained to all levels of employees, each of whom should receive a copy.

One example of a company's approach to a code of ethics is Brunswick Corporation, which makes its code of ethics (in five languages) available on its web site and on paper not only to guide its employees at all levels but also to be read by shareholders, customers, and suppliers. Brunswick's code discusses the main issues of concern such as conflicts of interest, fraud, gifts, harassment, proprietary information, e-mail, and insider activities. The topics are illustrated with generic examples to enhance understanding of the principle involved.

INTERNAL CONTROLS

Another requirement under the new law is that management must identify and assess the risk of fraudulent financial reporting within its own operations and the adequacy of its internal controls. That means reviewing the existing environment as a starting point. This review should have the character of what has become known as a forensic audit, in which the company, typically with the assistance of expert consultants, looks for weaknesses and opportunities for fraud.

It should be noted that a review cannot be avoided simply by pointing to a recent clean audit opinion. That opinion is irrelevant as far as Sarbanes-Oxley is concerned, because the traditional audit was never designed to review internal controls in the manner now expected. Nor can management sit and wait for the external auditor to tell it what is needed, because setting up the system is management's responsibility. Only after these steps have been taken will the external auditors come in to attest to, and report on, the assessment made by the management.

What exactly might good internal controls entail? COSO's seminal 1987 "Report of the National Commission on Fraudulent Financial Reporting" (known as the Treadway Report) looked to the Federal Corrupt Practices Act of 1977 for a definition of what assurances an effective system of internal controls should provide to ensure that transactions are not fraudulent. It said that transactions must be authorized by management and recorded in such a way as to permit preparation of financial statements and an accounting of assets. Only management should be able to authorize access to assets and a physical count should periodically be made and compared with the record.

But just having management oversight is not sufficient. The 1999 COSO report on fraudulent financial reporting found that of the nearly 300 cases studied, the CEO and CFO either alone or in collusion were associated with 83 percent of the frauds. These cases show how important it is for the responsibilities of the senior officers to be strictly segregated. For example, the CEO should not act as the CFO. Spending limits and signing authorities must be clearly defined.

Of course, the real question is how well these controls are enforced. Unfortunately, studies of fraud cases brought to the attention of the SEC between 1981 and 1986 showed that the executive power to override controls was also a consistent factor in frauds. The Association of Certified Fraud Examiners has also found in its research that the opportunity for executives to override controls is a serious threat. This threat must be addressed by each company in the context of its own corporate structure.

The expanded role of the audit committee is intended to help address this issue. Although it varies from company to company, the audit committee's role as to internal audit and monitoring of CEO/CFO activity must include a review of the effectiveness of internal controls and the internal audit function. The committee must also review management and the company's code of conduct at least annually. It is one thing to have a code of conduct, it is another to review it regularly and enforce it.

INTERNAL AUDIT

An effective internal audit function, with adequate staff to carry it out, is an essential part of any internal control system. The internal audit team should have the full support of senior management, the board of directors, and the audit committee.

The integrity and impartiality of the chief internal auditor and the members of the team should be beyond question. The chief internal auditor should report to a senior officer not involved in the production of financial statements and should have direct access to the CEO and the chair of the audit committee at all times.

The internal auditor brings a detailed operational knowledge that should be coordinated with the work of the external auditor to develop antifraud controls. Companies must not become overly reliant on the internal auditor to detect fraud, however.

Of the 663 known fraud cases studied by the members of the Association of Certified Fraud Examiners for its 2002 report, internal audit teams were responsible for discovering only 18.6 percent, while mere chance turned up 18.8 percent. Notably, tips from employees revealed 26.3 percent. Thus, the internal audit must be seen as only one of the internal antifraud controls. Honest employees inspired by ethical business practices and protected by new whistleblower legislation under Sarbanes-Oxley should be encouraged to play their role as part of the internal control system.

This is also the area where corporate security can have the greatest impact. For example, many security professionals are responsible for internal investigations of suspected fraud and for making recommendations to internal audit personnel regarding improvements in safeguarding assets. Corporate security also may be responsible for setting up and overseeing an employee hotline.

COMMON PROBLEMS

The most common problems that I have encountered when reviewing clients' internal controls since Sarbanes-Oxley became law involve failure: failure to segregate conflicting duties, failure to reconcile accounts, failure to have these reconciliations reviewed by someone independent of the reconciliation process, and failure to do follow-ups to make sure problems get solved.

In some cases, these problems are uncovered when the company itself recognizes that a problem has occurred that must be fixed before senior management and the external auditors can attest to the effectiveness of internal controls. For example, a distributor had been growing rapidly through the acquisition of distribution centers in several states. After a year or so of expanded operations, an unexplained inventory shortfall in excess of $30 million was discovered during a routine internal audit.

Detailed interviews with accounting personnel in the home office and at the newly acquired companies showed a range of perceptions as to how intercompany transfers were to be handled. A $20,000 transfer from inventory would be recorded as $20,000 in internal sales; however, perhaps only $15,000 worth of inventory was actually shipped and recorded as a $15,000 intercompany payable by the recipient. No one had called to check that the amount received was the amount sent or to question why there was a discrepancy.

By the time my firm was called, millions of dollars of inventory needed to be reconciled and explained. So many problems had been outstanding for so long that management could not tell whether arithmetic errors, sloppy recordkeeping, or fraud had created the discrepancies.

We recommended tighter inventory controls, more frequent communication between the shipping and receiving companies, and better documentation in the form of shipping and receiving slips. Reconciliations are now made monthly and any differences are investigated and reconciled immediately.

Another company had experienced several embezzlements and, while management believed the problems were behind them, they chose to have an independent examination of their internal controls to satisfy the audit committee. We found that the problem had concerned one employee in the accounting department who was making the most of conflicting responsibilities. She not only received the bills from suppliers but also had the authority to generate manual checks to pay them.

Because no one was reconciling the bills with the checks, this employee created a few false accounts and wrote checks to herself. After the fraud was revealed, the company introduced a more effective reconciliation process, imposed another layer of oversight, and began to generate all checks by computer.

In the 18 months following the discovery of the fraud, the company had made great strides in tightening its internal controls overall. However, during the same period, the company had expanded, creating potential problems because some of the company's accounting functions were being conducted at the home office, while many others were decentralized. That arrangement had advantages and disadvantages. The biggest advantage was that collusion to commit fraud would be very difficult. The challenge for the company, however, was to maintain a balance of decentralization and control without making the reporting process so time consuming that people would try to circumvent it.

Many companies face that same challenge as they seek to develop good internal controls. The bottom line under Sarbanes-Oxley is that whatever approach they take, top management will now be under the watchful eye of more independent boards and external auditors—and will be held directly accountable for their company's financial statements.

NOTE

1. This chapter originally appeared as "The Importance of Being Earnest," *Security Management Magazine*, February 2004, Howard Silverstone, CPA.

4

PROACTIVE FRAUD INVESTIGATIONS: AN INTRODUCTION

FRAUD INVESTIGATIONS DEFINED

Traditionally, proactive fraud investigations, and indeed an element of reactive fraud investigations, have been referred to as "fraud auditing." Fraud auditing has been considered a unique specialty that involves the use of auditing techniques developed for the sole purpose of detecting evidence of fraud. There have traditionally been two stages to fraud auditing, each of which requires a different operating methodology by the auditor as well as a different mind-set: the proactive stage and the reactive stage.

What is a little confusing about fraud auditing is that by using the word audit, it may imply that the investigation is not as thorough or invasive as a fraud investigation should be. For purposes of this text, we would like to discuss the concept of fraud investigations as opposed to fraud auditing.

As implausible as the analogy may be, the practice of proactive fraud investigations is not unlike the practice of medical doctors who examine their patients for signs of malignancies, solely because they are in special risk categories, even though the patients appear to be in good health and have no symptoms. Basically, this is what proactive fraud investigators do. They examine entities at risk of fraud but that have no obvious symptoms that fraud has occurred. The intensity of a proactive fraud investigation is based on the degree to which an entity is at risk, not on any evident symptoms of fraud. The reactive investigator's job essentially begins when they have discovered indications—often called indicia—that fraud may be present. Returning to the analogy involving medical doctors, this is quite similar to the physician who discovers a suspicious lump in a patient. The discovery often means nothing by itself, but it is usually sufficient reason for the doctor to investigate further.

At the point of the detection, however, the nature of the doctor's examination changes from a relatively blind examination of areas at risk to a very specific examination of the detected lump or nodule. He or she is likely to perform specific tests to determine the nature of the finding. So it is with the reactive investigator. With the detection of indicia of fraud, the investigator changes the nature of his or her examination from a blind search for indicia to a specific search for evidence that will validate whether the fraud indicia discovered is malignant or benign.

Although the practice of medicine has many doctors qualified to assist their patients, the comparison ends there. While Enron, WorldCom, and other fraud scandals have led to Sarbanes-Oxley, the Public Company Accounting Oversight Board, and the introduction of SAS 99, there are still far too few qualified professionals to practice fraud investigations adequately.

Fraud investigations generally have been thought of as a specialty of the general practice of internal auditing because they historically were practiced mostly by internal auditors, if at all. However, with the recent issues in the corporate and accounting world, companies are now forced to invest proactively not only in more and better internal standards, but also in outside resources. Given the proper circumstances, fraud investigations could and should be performed by independent certified public accountants (CPAs) and/or Certified Fraud Examiners (CFEs) on behalf of clients interested in the benefits of the investigation. The association of internal investigations with internal auditing undoubtedly

results from the greater freedom from regulation that internal auditors enjoy in performing their audits. Whereas CPAs must perform
in accordance with generally accepted auditing standards published
by the American Institute of Certified Public Accountants (AICPA),
and now within the fee limits set by Sarbanes-Oxley (standards
that, in effect, preclude fraud investigations), internal auditors are
not similarly restrained, at least not from a regulatory standpoint.
However, fraud investigations are generally not practiced by internal auditors, although they appear to have a strong interest in doing
so. Furthermore, many internal auditors who do seek out fraud are
not always provided with the necessary resources or freedom to engage in the practice to the degree they would like, and their opportunities for learning the skills needed are limited. Also, many
employers, complacent in their belief that they are fraud-free and/or
have adequate protection by virtue of their periodic independent
audits by CPA firms, make a grievous error, in the interests of cost
cutting, by restricting internal auditing resources that might otherwise be better spent on proactive fraud-specific investigations.

With the advent of Sarbanes-Oxley and the required certifications by the CEO and CFO, this is no longer true of public companies. In addition, Auditing Standard No. 2 issued by the Public
Company Accounting Oversight Board, "An Audit of Internal Control Over Financial Reporting Performed in Conjunction with an
Audit of Financial Statements," requires the external auditor to
evaluate the process management used to perform its assessment of
internal control effectiveness, evaluate the effectiveness of both the
design and operation of the internal control, and form an opinion
about whether internal control over financial reporting is effective.[1]

However, private companies may still not have heeded the
clarion call. While SAS 99 applies to their auditors, the corporate
governance over management is less defined and less stringent.
Internal auditors normally perform a widely diversified, somewhat nondiscretionary mix of activities, ranging from routine
obligations to ensure entity compliance with internal control

requirements to entity operational auditing. Although undoubtedly some entities have internal auditors with the resources and interests to be aggressive in proactive fraud investigations, such firms probably are in the minority.

THREE OBJECTIVES OF FRAUD INVESTIGATIONS

Fraud investigations have three basic objectives:

1. In the proactive stage, to search competently and persistently for indicia of fraud. The hunt for evidence continues to the point when the internal auditor or investigator is reasonably confident that he or she may have discovered fraud, or feels that sufficient testing has been done. In a more practical vein, investigators must stop searching when time runs out.

2. In the reactive stage, to search for validating evidence. To react to any indicative evidence discovered in the proactive stage. Also, if found, to compile the evidence necessary to be reasonably certain the investigator has discovered fraud and to support prosecution. In the reactive stage, if the investigator is not sufficiently trained or experienced in criminal investigations, he or she is advised to join with a criminal investigator to develop the necessary evidence to support prosecution.

3. To deter fraud by increasing the likelihood of detection.

The first objective is to search for evidence of fraud. Although detecting fraud is the intention of proactive investigations, it should never be the measure of audit efficiency. Whether or not evidence of fraud is detected, it should never be a criterion of how effective the work was or how well it was conducted. A "no fraud" result is just as valid as a "fraud" result.

At the outset of the first stage, the work usually begins from point zero, with nothing in the way of fraud evidence to guide the investigation. While many investigations start with some inkling of a problem, usually the only guidance is a survey of the entity and any operational areas the survey may have highlighted as being at a higher risk of fraud. These generally draw the investigator's initial attention. This is, without question, the most difficult stage of such an investigation.

When performing proactive investigations, the work normally begins in areas selected at the discretion of the investigator/auditor in conjunction with management, with no guidance regarding any fraud that actually may have occurred. They must look for evidence that has not yet become apparent and that may never become apparent. Their main concern is to remain alert to the faintest indicia of fraud. In some ways, without an incident that spurs an investigation, such work is like that of fishermen who stand for hours casting a hook at the end of a line into the water, patiently waiting for a successful strike. The fact that any given day is a bad fishing day does not deter them. Ask any fisherman. Eventually they will have the thrill of the catch, which will make all the unproductive days worthwhile.

Contrary to the popular impression that a case of fraud is readily evident when encountered by auditors, many if not most cases begin with the detection of a single clue and end as a collection of bits of evidence that all had to be found and assembled individually, any one of which was likely to be indistinguishable as evidence of fraud when first seen individually. If fraud investigators are tired, or rushing through their search, they might easily miss minuscule clues and not detect the case. The first bits of evidence often indicate or prove nothing by themselves, except to suggest—to the trained eye—the possibility of fraud, and that a search for additional evidence is a viable course of action.

PROACTIVE FRAUD INVESTIGATIONS

The proactive stage often involves two indistinct stages, which could be described as the pre-discovery stage, and the post-discovery stage. Where there are two stages, the latter stage occurs as the result of the discovery of some indication of fraud, but it is so weak that the investigator is unsure whether or not it constitutes indicia of fraud. In this post-discovery stage, a reactive criminal investigation is not usually suggested, as the case at this point is based on little more than suspicions. Instead, the proactive audit should be continued to search for additional confirming evidence. If no additional evidence of fraud is discovered, the finding is typically dropped. If sufficient additional evidence is found to support the suspicions, the case will enter the reactive phase. In the post-discovery stage, the company and its investigators will attempt to envision what sort of fraud is suggested by the evidence discovered. These stages involve the use of methods very much like the procedure followed when working a jigsaw puzzle. Once a picture is envisioned, missing pieces that fit the envisioned image are easier to look for and find. When a possible fraud is envisioned, search programs can be designed to look efficiently for the exact sort of evidence needed to either validate or nullify the suspected fraud. This technique is often called end auditing. The method is not always successful, but it is better than searching for validating clues without having at least an idea of what is being sought. At this point even though they have anticipated what the fraud may be, the investigator still doesn't have a solid lead, only a distinct feeling of being on a hot trail.

If the search produces sufficient validating evidence that seems to enhance the probability of fraud, investigators will schedule it for reactive audit development work. Investigators are well aware that many of the leads discovered in this stage of the work (and the fraud cases visualized when the first evidence was found) will die from a failure to discover further validating evidence. Of course, this fact does not mean that the initial clue was not an indicator of fraud—only that no additional evidence could be discovered.

Deciding when a proactive case becomes a reactive one is a matter of judgment and is likely to vary from case to case, depending on personal experience. The decision of further work and referral often depends on how large and dollar significant a case may be, and what paralegal and investigative skills the investigators have or can call upon. Of course, all good investigators are a bit paranoid. To them, the fact that they failed to find additional evidence to support their initial observations oftentimes only means that either the perpetrator was very clever and did not leave an evidence trail or that they missed finding it.

Less experienced investigators prolong preliminary casework unnecessarily, thereby delaying entry of skilled criminal investigators and/or prosecution counsel. It is always desirable for criminal investigators to be brought on the scene on a timely basis to take necessary affidavits from witnesses while their memories are fresh, and before critical evidence is lost or destroyed. Early assistance from prosecutors is highly desirable if it appears that the case is likely to be prosecuted, in order to assure that continuing audit/investigative work is relevant to case requirements.

Many private and governmental entities have a system that allows employees and others to anonymously report irregularities, some of which turn out to be fraudulent. Indeed among the many obligations created for public companies by the Sarbanes-Oxley Act, is the requirement to implement a hotline for confidential and anonymous complaints to the audit committee from whistleblowing employees. Such confidential tips, noted elsewhere in this book as the primary way in which frauds are initially detected,[2] normally are received with little or no documentation and very few particulars. However, they should never be ignored and they must be considered for follow-up.

CASE   4.1 The Office Supply Store Fraud

One large government fraud case began with a barely legible hand-scribbled note that was mailed to the U.S. General Services Administration by the jilted girlfriend of one of the perpetrators. The note described how her ex-lover—the manager of an office supply store—was involved in criminal activity, and how he had been cheating on her with another woman. When the note was received, the first reaction was to ignore it as the product of a rejected lover attempting to make trouble for the man who rejected her. However, the lead was taken seriously, and it turned out to be the loose thread that unraveled a widespread fraud in federal office supply stores across the country.

Typical of the many frauds that were uncovered was a scheme that involved office supply brokers who would visit store managers and propose a conspiracy to commit fraud. Interestingly, they had many takers. The visiting broker would propose that store managers purchase merchandise that would never be delivered—perhaps something like $5,000 in ballpoint pens. If the store manager agreed, and many did, he or she would issue a purchase order to the broker, who would then generate all the necessary paperwork that would accompany a legitimate order and shipment of merchandise, including shipping documents and an invoice—but no merchandise. The store manager would process the invoice, certifying that the merchandise had been received, and the invoice amount would be paid to the broker. Subsequently, the broker and the store manager would divide the cash received. The retail inventory method in effect at the time at the stores facilitated the fraud by not highlighting irregularities in specific items in store inventories, such as the ballpoint pens, but would spread the inventory shortages out over the entire merchandise line, diminishing its apparent significance. This fraud case would have been difficult to prove without the woman's report. Adding to detection difficulty was the fact that store managers also had considerable latitude in setting unit sales prices. Accordingly, they would increase the prices of legitimate items being sold to increase sales revenue, which in turn tended to cover the shortages. The case eventually was prosecuted successfully due to the excessive greed of the perpetrators and an abundance of evidence discovered.

Reactive Fraud Investigations

Reactive investigations consist of searching for and compiling the evidence necessary to support prosecution. The term reactive is derived from the fact that people literally are reacting to validated evidence of fraud discovered in the proactive stage, or from some other source, and are setting an examination path that focuses on the evidence to which they are reacting. As more and more evidence is discovered (or not discovered) the path varies depending on any new case insights gained. Often mitigating circumstances that tend to negate the presumptions of fraud are discovered in the reactive stage of an audit or investigation. Investigators should keep open minds regarding this possibility. Remember, a no fraud result *is* a valid conclusion.

Usually the difference between proactive and reactive work is clear. When examining proactively, investigators initially have no indications of the type of fraud that may be present, and follow procedures designed to detect evidence to confirm or deny speculation. Once an indication of fraud is detected, regardless of how slight, suspicions are enhanced but the existence of fraud is still not certain. However, when validating evidence is discovered and everyone becomes convinced the case being pursued is a bona-fide fraud discovery, the investigation tends to change to a reactive one. Further procedures are designed to concentrate on those factors that will improve the prosecutorial worth of the finding. Such factors include determining who the perpetrators are, whether other cases involving the perpetrators have occurred previously, proving the suspects' intent to commit fraud, and determining the total loss to the victim resulting from the fraud.

The roles of proactive and criminal investigators are also reasonably clear. Criminal investigators rarely work proactively to discover fraud. They almost always begin their investigative tasks with a request from the victim, who has either come by evidence of fraud or has strong suspicions of fraud that he or she wishes to be investigated. These suspicions include requests from proactive investigators who require assistance after concluding that sufficient evidence has been accumulated to indicate the possibility of fraud.

Depending on case circumstances, often this referral point is delayed to keep the fraud finding confidential. Regrettably, once criminal investigators begin their work, any confidentiality of the discovery of fraud is usually lost. Any time such investigators are present, it usually indicates a suspected criminal act, and the office gossip begins. An entity's employee population becomes quickly accustomed to the presence of proactive auditors who are searching for evidence of fraud that may not exist, and they rarely attribute their presence to the detection of fraud. Howerver, by the time criminal investigators come on the scene, most employees realize that the situation has changed and thus they can't help but discuss it. In addition, investigators usually interview suspects and potential witnesses, and ask pointed questions regarding the suspected fraud. Sworn statements are also usually taken, which leaves office onlookers with little doubt as to the specifics of the crime and the probable suspects. The danger here, of course, is that innocent or unproven suspects will be defamed, which is why investigative procedures should not be started prematurely.

The reactive stage of fraud investigations is also marked by a new perspective on the job to be done. That is, with evidence of fraud in hand, the review team focuses on gathering the necessary evidence to prosecute the suspected perpetrator(s) successfully.

They seek to obtain corroborating evidence. If the case is dollar significant and difficult, the team should enlist the assistance of other team members who have criminal investigative and/or legal (prosecution) experience, and who can proceed without alarming the office community.

Readers are advised not to be overconfident when seeking prosecution. Having a case declined by a prosecutor for lack of evidence is a frustrating experience, especially when auditors have collected what they believe to be overwhelming evidence of fraud. The following case relates such an experience.

CASE 4.2   Trucking Firm Engages in Defective Delivery Fraud

One such case that was nearly lost due to a lack of the right sort of evidence involved a trucking firm that had a contract to deliver supplies from a government warehouse to various government agencies in the Chicago area. The firm skimmed merchandise from large deliveries over a period of time. Apparently people at the firm noticed that some customers did not check the quantities of merchandise delivered and so they took small quantities of merchandise from each delivery to those particular customers. When they had accumulated a truckload of stolen goods from this skimming practice, they would deliver it to a dealer in stolen merchandise. There were no apparent suspicions that these thefts were taking place, in that no customers had reported any shortages in the merchandise received. However, as sometimes happens, fate intervened. In this case, fate arrived in the form of a significant snowstorm.

During the snowstorm, a truck laden with stolen government property was found abandoned on a Chicago street that had been designated a vital snow route and where parking was prohibited during snowstorms. To clear the street, the Chicago police had the truck towed to a police lot, where it was later examined, and the government property was discovered. The federal police who investigated found it simple to trace the trailer's registration to the trucking firm involved. There was no doubt that the trucking firm had engaged in criminal fraud, and shortly after, the case was presented to the U.S. attorney's office for prosecution. Tried before a federal judge, the trucker was found guilty. However, after the trial, the U.S. assistant attorney who prosecuted the case told the auditors that the judge involved had great reservations about the case. Apparently he had little, if any, doubt that the defendant was guilty but was uncomfortable with the prosecutor's scant demonstration of the trucking company's intent to defraud the government. He was uncomfortable in concluding intent—a prerequisite for conviction—from the one truckload of stolen merchandise that was presented as evidence. Upon reflection, the investigation should have sought evidence that this trucker had practiced this particular fraud on prior occasions. Apparently the judge wanted to see this; undoubtedly such information would have been a factor in sentencing the defendant.

Deterring Fraud by Increasing Risk of Detection

Perhaps the most significant objective of proactive fraud investigation is the internal control effect that it establishes, if done properly. Regardless of how unsuccessful a proactive fraud examination may be in detecting fraud indicia, it can always serve as a deterrent if the work is done visibly and if it is performed in areas that fraud perpetrators may be considering. Fraud investigations that are done well put an unavoidable and often intolerable risk into the practice of perpetrating fraud. Most (if not all) fraudsters do not want to be caught. In those cases in which an entity fails to practice routine proactive checks, would-be fraud perpetrators are assured that, if they are careful and plan their fraudulent acts well, they run a minimal risk of discovery. However, if fraud avoidance efforts—particularly proactive auditing efforts—are expended periodically across a wide spectrum of an entity's operations, regardless of the purpose of the searches or their success in detecting fraud indicia, would-be and actual perpetrators will be on notice that any perpetration in those areas runs the risk of detection. Where there is little or no risk, only moral restraints keep people with few or no moral values from the easy money. Even though routine fraud examination may fail to detect any evidence of fraud, practice proactive investigation anyway. The risk of detection it imposes just may deter a would-be perpetrator.

The twentieth century posed few insurmountable obstacles to fraud. Few effective proactive investigations were performed and would-be perpetrators surely were encouraged by the low risk of detection. In contemplating fraud, it is relatively easy for a perpetrator to become aware of the internal controls in effect and to find ways and means of avoiding them. Many internal controls are relatively naive and especially ineffective when conspiracy is part of the scheme. Frequently, even skilled investigators do not find fraud that is cleverly hidden, so deterrence becomes a main objective of the review. Contrary to what some criminologists suggest, most fraud perpetrators do not wish to be caught and are very cautious. However, the presence of skilled fraud investigators who periodically comb through transactions constitutes an ever-present threat and will probably deter all bu the most determined perpetrators.

ADVICE FOR INEXPERIENCED FRAUD INVESTIGATORS

Beginning fraud investigators should follow five rules:

1. **Avoid** becoming prematurely entangled in developing endless facts and circumstances of a case of fraud to the exclusion of identifying a perpetrator or perpetrators and proving their involvement. As puzzling as this suggestion may appear at first,

many investigators become obsessed with developing the interesting details of a fraud case and tend to forget why they are doing what they are doing. Many fully document sensational details of a fraud case, then, when they are asked "Who did it?" cannot answer.

Most investigators are basically nice people who feel comfortable with the impersonal aspects of their work. When describing incidents of waste, for example, most internal audit reports fail to mention who was responsible for the waste being reported. In fact, the Office of Auditing of the U.S. General Services Administration (GSA) once experimented with putting the names of people who had knowledge of but were not the guilty parties of the events described in their audit reports, and the practice drew an angry reaction. Accordingly, internal auditors tend to be trained to report a finding on the order of "There is inadequate underlying support for the $12,000 payment to the Jones Company," without ever determining the names of the people who were responsible; they seem to consider that an irrelevant personal detail. During a lecture, a group of mid-level managers and auditors of an international corporation were told that, in pursuing a fraud examination, they must identify a list of perpetrator suspects as early as possible in the examination, and examine all the transactions those people may have been involved in. Several of those in attendance remarked that they would have difficulty intruding into the affairs of innocent people. They were asked if they ever heard of the expression "Nice guys finish last." Fraud does not just happen of its own accord. Someone is always involved. Accordingly, once you find the first indicia of fraud, you must begin to consider who the perpetrators are likely to be.

2. Fraud investigators must constantly strive to prove a perpetrator's intent to commit fraud. Countless fraud cases in the discovered but never prosecuted category are there and will

remain there because some auditor or investigator failed to prove clearly who did the crime and that the accused perpetrator intended to commit fraud. Proving an accused perpetrator's intent to commit the crime he or she is accused of is often extremely difficult, but it is an absolutely necessary requirement for prosecution in the courts. Without a clear demonstration of intent, a case is not likely to be prosecuted, regardless of the weight of evidence regarding the crime itself. The purpose of the courts is to judge people, not to hear detail-rich stories of the crimes involved. In addition, if a company chooses to file a fidelity (dishonesty) bond claim, the bonding company will need to be shown direct evidence that the person committed the scheme and that they or an accomplice obtained direct financial benefit.

3. Be creative, think like a perpetrator, and do not be predictable. When searching for evidence of fraud, particularly when proactively searching, fraud investigators have considerable license to vary search methods, objectives, parameters, and locations. Some of the most successful discoveries have been achieved by people who literally asked themselves "What would a perpetrator do in a situation such as this?" and then proceeded to test whether they were correct.

The U.S. General Services Administration (GSA) used to have an internal control requirement that all contracts $200,000 and over had to be examined by internal auditors for any obvious improprieties. Predictably, few if any exceptions ever were discovered. However, one day an auditor, while proactively searching for evidence of fraud, decided that any serious perpetrators would most likely be aware of the $200,000 internal control requirement. Thus, if they were going to attempt fraud, it would be more likely in contracts just under $200,000. Accordingly, the auditors decided to lower the audit threshold to $150,000 without notice. The result: multiple infractions were discovered, many of them easily found and obviously intentional, surely because perpetrators expected that the auditors would not examine the contracts. Obviously the internal audits had been painfully predictable.

4. Fraud detection procedures must take into account that many times fraud involves conspiracy—either true conspiracy or pseudo-conspiracy. Many internal control systems are designed to prevent unauthorized acts by people acting alone. However, few if any internal control systems can prevent illegal acts by two or more people acting as co-conspirators to evade the internal controls.

Accordingly, when planning a fraud discovery strategy, although you must consider the fraud-specific efficacy of the internal controls in place, you should not depend on them excessively. At one time conspiracies by two or more people were rare, and auditors depended heavily on that assumption. Collusion is no longer rare, and auditors must learn to depend far less on internal controls designed to prevent people who are acting alone from committing fraud. Adding to the investigators' dilemma is the fact that many perpetrators have discovered that individuals charged with maintaining internal controls are often negligent or poorly trained, and can be tricked into failures equivalent to lowering fraud barriers. Accordingly, it is appropriate to classify collusion into two categories, conspiracy and pseudo-conspiracy:

a. Ordinary conspiracy involves the willing cooperation of two or more people intent on committing fraud.

b. Pseudo-conspiracy occurs when one or more of the people cooperating in the fraud scheme is innocent of any intent to commit fraud, or has no knowledge of the fraud scheme, but fails to act (or acts in a negligent manner) so as to make fraud by another person or persons possible. Pseudo-conspirators are never aware that they are a party to fraud and have no intent to commit criminal acts. Pseudo-conspiracies often occur, for example, when per-

petrators evade internal controls by enlisting the cooperation of an innocent person who is responsible for maintaining the control feature. Usually the innocent party is
somehow tricked into cooperating. Most frequently this occurs when entities employing pseudo-conspirators do not
select and train key internal control employees adequately,
and/or do not refresh their training often enough.

Similar internal control lapses also are likely to occur
during vacations, sick outages, days off, and rest breaks
when temporary personnel replace regular experienced
control clerks. The following case illustrates the cost of
negligence.

CASE 4.3   The Negligent Internal Control Clerk

The following actual fraud, involving a pseudo-conspiracy,
totaled over $900,000 and required the participation of an in-
ternal control register clerk in a large automated payment
system. The automated system involved was designed to accept only transactions that were submitted by authorized
people. To demonstrate that they were permitted to use the
system, all authorized users authenticated their accounting
documents submitted for processing by including the lowest
unused number from a series of ascending numbers issued
only to them. Each number could be used only once and,
when used in ascending order, assured the processing system
that the person submitting them was approved and that all
transactions submitted had been processed—and no more.
No duplicate numbers would be accepted, and any missing
numbers resulted in a search for the missing documents. The
system seemed reasonably secure and, theoretically at least,
precluded unauthorized people from using the system. Any

possible payment fraud would be limited to a small circle of authorized users. However, the key to the control system was the clerk who was in charge of issuing the blocks of control numbers to authorized users.

From time to time, a friendly and charismatic man-about-the-office who had gained the friendship and trust of many employees explained to the clerk that one of the authorized system users had asked him to pick up a new block of numbers for him. Not realizing the significance of issuing the control numbers only to authorized users, the clerk would comply and issue a block of numbers logged to whoever the man named. The man subsequently used the numbers to submit phony documents for building maintenance services that allowed him to steal over $900,000.

The innocent control number clerk became a pseudo-conspirator when she gave out the control numbers and, in so doing, made the man's fraud possible. The clerk had no knowledge of the fraud scheme or the man's criminal intent, and so was not guilty of a criminal act. She was not even found to be negligent because her employer could not demonstrate that she had been adequately trained or refreshed as to the internal security significance of the control numbers.

In other instances similar to this one, even though control clerks may, in fact, be adequately trained in the internal control role, occasionally they are absent. Whether for vacation time, sick absences, lunch breaks, coffee breaks, or rest periods, substitute clerks must be assigned, and all of them must be trained adequately if the control system is to work effectively. Alert perpetrators will watch for undertrained, careless, insecure, or underattentive clerks and take advantage of any lapse in control.

---

5. Proactive fraud detection strategy must consider that fraud may appear in the accounting records as distinct entries or hosted entries and, in some instances, it may not appear in the records at all.

Some fraud, though not a lot, appears in accounting records as distinct accounting entries. Multiple-payment fraud, duplicate-payment fraud, and shell fraud are all examples of fraud cases that involve distinct entries. If a fraud investigator randomly selects a fraudulent entry to be tested, the entire amount of the transaction will be the amount of the fraud, and discovery is likely. Distinct accounting fraud is perhaps the simplest of the three to discover.

Assume that a random audit test includes a $5,000 payment to ABC Contractors for construction work. The auditor discovers that the entire item contracted for is a total fabrication. It was never delivered by ABC Contractors. Further investigation reveals that the transaction is fraudulent. The entire $5,000 will be the amount of the fraud. There will be no legitimate support whatsoever for the disbursement. There is nothing to justify the payment, no question as to the amount of the fraud or who is responsible.

A lot of fraud that occurs is hosted entry fraud. When it occurs, the amount of the fraud is masked by an apparently legitimate transaction that hosts it. Accordingly, if auditors select, at random, a payment for $50,000 for 1,000 widgets, they may find what appears to be a perfectly proper payment. The paperwork is all correct, and all 1,000 widgets appear to have been received, signed for, and placed in inventory. Do the auditors pass the transaction as being fraud free? Not necessarily. At least several different frauds are possible, despite the audit tests performed.

Although the receiving records indicate that 1,000 widgets have been received, in fact, fewer may actually have been received. Or, the transaction examined may have been the second of two—the first legitimate, the second fraudulent. In both cases there would be a legitimate order for 1,000 widgets at $50,000, which would pass most audit tests. It would be confirmed that all 1,000 widgets had been received, and all the paperwork would have passed ordinary scrutiny. Only in the unlikely event that auditors happen to select both transactions would the fraud become obvious, and even then it would be unlikely. The legitimate entry would, in effect, host and mask the illegitimate entry.

A kickback is another example of fraud that is hosted by an otherwise legitimate transaction. The kickback amounts are always included in the price the victim pays for the product or service received. In such contracts, auditors reviewing contract details would find that a properly authorized and legitimate product or service was delivered. The only problem would be in determining whether the price was right. In many cases this is a very difficult determination. Subsequent chapters discuss ethical issues, including kickback fraud, and suggest audit and internal control techniques for dealing with it.

Another type of fraud is that which is off the books. Inexperienced investigators must note that selecting transactions for examination from the accounting records does not always uncover all fraud that may have occurred. Consider accounts receivable that have been written off as bad debts and subsequently collected. A perpetrator has the opportunity to divert payments for bad debts with no record on the books that the debt had been paid. Scrap inventories that were never capitalized can be another type of off-the-books fraud. Frequently, manufacturers generate scrap inventories that have considerable value. If those scrap inventories are sold without having been capitalized, the revenue from the sales could be diverted and never appear on the accounting records for auditors who did not go beyond the accounting records in their search for fraud. For example, one organization followed the practice of reclaiming the silver content from discarded X-ray films. Occasionally the considerable silver that was collected would disappear. No examination of accounting transactions would ever disclose the theft. No one could ever say with certainty the value of the inventory that may have been stolen. Ultimately, the theft was deterred by periodically capitalizing the silver inventories that were generated.

NOTES

1. Public Company Accounting Oversight Board, www.pcaobus.org/default .asp.
2. Association of Certified Fraud Examiners, "2004 Report to the Nation on Occupational Fraud and Abuse."

5

PROACTIVE FRAUD INVESTIGATIONS: CONDUCTING THE INVESTIGATION

Proactive fraud-specific investigations bear few similarities to traditional audits. To understand fully what such investigations are and are not, traditional auditing practices also must be understood. In the simplest terms possible, it is fair to say that whereas traditional auditing seeks to verify things that are known to be, proactive fraud-specific investigations seek to determine the existence of things that are not known to be and may not be.

Admittedly, this simple definition sounds very much like a riddle, and will be explained in the paragraphs that follow. However, using the old clichéd analogy of the needle and the haystack, consider how each type of auditor would react if the haystack were somehow involved in his or her audit objective. Whereas traditional auditors would be likely to look upon the haystack and see only a need to verify the quantity of hay in the stack, proactive fraud investigators would likely ignore the quantity of the hay and ponder, instead, how to find the needle(s) that might be in it. Although neither type spends much time looking at haystacks, the illustration depicts the mind-set and objectives each takes in his or her endeavors and the relative difficulty each auditor faces in accomplishing those objectives.

Determining the amount of hay in the stack is a relatively

straightforward task. Auditors begin with something tangible. There are no doubts that it exists. All that is left for them to do is measure it and perhaps test it; both tasks are very doable. However, determining whether there is one or more needles in the haystack and finding it or them is obviously a much more difficult task, and requires methods quite different from those employed by traditional auditors. To begin with, there is no tangible evidence to suggest that the fraud—the needle—actually exists. Also, most of the time no evidence is ever found that it did exist. However, there is also no evidence that it does not exist. Accordingly, fraud investigators frequently search for things that, most of the time, simply are not there. In fact, if they could be assured that they were searching for something as tangible as needles, their job would be greatly simplified.

There are, however, methods proactive investigators can use to maximize their fraud detection probabilities. In the following sections, readers should note the differences between proactive fraud investigation techniques and traditional auditing; and they should attempt to understand why traditional auditors, particularly independent ones, cannot possibly be expected to accomplish dual audit objectives. They cannot actively search for indicia of fraud while conducting ongoing verifications of financial statement balances or attempt to accomplish routine audit tasks without a significant increase in resources and time expended. In fact, independent auditors attempting to perform proactive fraud-specific audits without the unique training and/or experience needed often find that their well-intentioned efforts at fraud detection are less than productive.

The great difficulty in proactive fraud investigations is that investigators are often working blind. The traditional audit normally begins with an assertion of some kind by the entity being audited that something—a financial statement balance or a condition—is correct. The traditional auditor's task is basically to verify that assertion. The proactive fraud investigator is not as fortunate. There are no assertions to be verified, other than the beginning presumption that there is no known fraud but fraud may exist.

> *A crime is like a fine omelet. You get your first clue of what's in it when you put your fork in it.*[1]

This is very much the case in proactive fraud investigations. You first must choose what to examine for fraud from the myriad of options that are available and then search for the clues that may signal the possibility that fraud is present. If you simply search for clues without specific agenda, chances of ever discovering fraud are minimal, if they exist at all.

ART OF FISHING

> *There are two types of fisherman—those who fish for sport and those who fish for fish.*[2]

The practice of proactive fraud investigation is like the art of fishing. It is very much an art in that detection success depends on the exercise of intuitive and creative talents. Whereas traditional auditors tend to be very methodical in their work—that is, left-brain oriented, relying on carefully considered generally accepted audit standards and tried-and-true audit procedures—experienced fraud investigators tend to be less inhibited in the conduct of their examinations and often rely substantially on their instincts and gut feelings; theirs is a right-brained orientation.

People who are not skilled fishermen think of fishing as a simple matter of hooking a worm, attaching the hook to the end of a line tied to a long pole, and dropping the hook into the water. It is possible to catch some fish this way, and many auditors search for fraud this way. But anyone who has done any serious fishing knows that this is not the way to maximize the catch or to catch the fish of choice. Fishermen actually begin by first deciding what type of fish they wish to catch. Most game fish require very different fishing methodologies, fishing locales, and fishing gear, and the fisherman who elects to catch any one type of fish is unlikely to catch any other type of fish using the same methods, equipment, and techniques. For example, the fisherman seeking to catch brook trout is unlikely to catch bass while fishing for brook trout.

> *Many men go fishing all of their lives without knowing that it is not fish they are after.*[3]

The same is very true of fraud. Fraud investigators must begin by selecting a type of fraud to attempt to detect. Once selected, a program is designed to detect the specific type of fraud selected, and only that type. Often the programs utilized are so specific to a particular type of fraud that the person is unlikely to detect any other type of fraud. For example, the auditor seeking to detect multiple payee fraud is unlikely to detect duplicate payment fraud, even though the latter fraud may be present in the transaction selected for examination.

There is one exception in the favorable comparison of fishing with proactive fraud investigations. In fishing, fishermen take pains not to scare the fish away. They want to catch fish, and quietly go about the sport. In searching for fraud, just the opposite is true. Fraud seekers may choose to make their investigations as visible as possible in order to scare fraud perpetrators away. If they can deter perpetrators from committing fraud with the threat of detection, the work can be said to have been successful.

> *There's a fine line between fishing and just standing on the shore like an idiot.*[4]

HOW PROACTIVE FRAUD INVESTIGATORS
THINK AND WORK

As an investigator, you must cultivate a mind-set that is different from that of traditional auditors. You must ignore all the rules you learned in practicing your craft. It is difficult to illustrate this without returning to a whimsical comparison on how both auditor types—using techniques learned in their auditing professions—would approach a fishing challenge. For example, assume that a traditional auditor and a fraud investigator both set out for a day of fishing. The objective of each is to catch as many walleye pike (a delicious freshwater fish) as possible. After arriving at the lake, the traditional auditor, influenced by customary audit methodology, proceeds to divide the lake into equal grid-like sections in order to eliminate any bias, and throughout the day, he fishes equally in each grid segment, carefully recording the number of walleye pike caught in each. This fisherman catches no fish. In fact, based on a statistical sample, calculated to provide a 98 percent confidence level, there were no walleye pike in the entire lake. This fisherman decides that it is futile to spend any more time fishing and goes home to feast on chicken.

The fraud investigator, on the other hand, influenced by a different methodology, is not interested in the numbers of walleye pike in the entire lake. She is interested only in catching enough for dinner that evening. Accordingly, she programs the search in such a manner as to maximize the chances of catching the wily pike. She does not search randomly in every part of the lake, as did the traditional auditor, because she knows that walleye pike do not inhabit all parts of the lake. Rather, she fishes only in those parts of the lake where she knows the walleye pike would be, if there were any. Doing this allows her to eliminate much of the center area of the lake, where she knows that the walleye pike spend little time. Why? She knows they have weak eyes and prefer the cooler, shady shorelines. She is also aware that the fish detest the bright sun and the heat of the day, and actively feed only in the early morning and late evening hours.

Whereas her friend the traditional auditor slept late and had a late breakfast, she got up at dawn and missed breakfast to be on the lake when the fish were feeding, thereby increasing her chances of catching fish. When she leaves the lake in midmorning, she has enough fish to feed her entire family. Note that the fraud investigator here eschewed statistical sampling and was totally biased in choosing locations and times of the day to maximize her catch.

Returning to the real world, whereas traditional auditors normally are concerned with confirming the overall value and/or condition of something, such as a reported inventory balance or reported accounts receivable, proactive fraud investigators are less concerned with confirming the accuracy of an inventory balance or accounts receivable balance reported than they would be with analyzing the transactions that enter into determining the inventory or accounts receivable balance. Traditional auditors, on the other hand, are minimally interested in the inventory transactions, as long as the value of the inventory reported to be on hand is materially correct. A determination that the inventory on hand may have been materially depleted as a result of fraud several months earlier is not an audit objective of traditional independent auditors. For example, an independent auditor engaged to verify a financial statement balance that included inventory reported to be worth $100 million would likely be satisfied if he or she were able to determine that the client actually possessed $100 million worth of goods. The auditor would be likely to overlook a $1 million discrepancy in the reported balance as being immaterial. A fraud investigator, on the other hand, is less concerned with the correctness of the $100 million balance reported because he or she knows that although correctly reported, it nevertheless could have been fraudulently depleted. This investigator would be very concerned with the $1 million inventory discrepancy.

Although both professionals routinely use statistical sampling, each is likely to use it somewhat differently. Traditional auditors make every effort to avoid bias in conducting and/or citing their audit testing to ensure that the final test results are representative of the whole. As a result, in their verification process usually they are willing to accept results with a predetermined confidence level of less than 100 percent—perhaps 95 to 98 percent. Fraud investigators are concerned that a determination of asset value through a statistical sampling process tends to eliminate any anomalies in the data universe that may be immaterial in terms of the total asset but that are of special interest to them. So-called anomalies may be the faint clues or fraud indicia that will lead them to the detection of fraud.

BEGINNING THE INVESTIGATION

One does not simply enter an employer's or client's office and begin looking for fraud. To begin searching for fraud proactively, one must select a specific type of fraud to hunt for. Some investigators are specialists and search for only one type of fraud. By concentrating on one type of fraud, they become experts at catching their quarry. Those who search for fraudulent insurance claims are one example.

Whichever variety of fish the fishermen may choose to fish for, they are well aware that it will require specific methods, special equipment, a special place to fish, and fishing only at certain hours of the day. If they are looking to catch trout, they know that only special gear suitable for catching trout will do. They also have to know where the trout are feeding (perhaps a pool of water off a fast-moving stream), when the trout are likely to be feeding, and on what. Also, fishermen know that if they are not careful, their mere presence in the area will alarm the fish and diminish their chances for catching any. In fact, even when fishermen have done everything correctly, there is no assurance that they will be successful.

Many fishermen believe that fish are wily creatures that possess a natural intelligence that allows them to survive.

Everything that fishermen must do to catch fish applies to proactive investigations. Investigators who simply search for fraud without having something specific in mind before beginning will not be very likely to find any fraud. Like fishermen, you must decide in advance of the search what type of fraud you are going to search for. It may be duplicate payment fraud, multiple payee fraud, shell fraud, defective delivery, defective shipment, defective pricing, contract rigging, unbalanced contracts, or any of dozens of others, including countless variations of those named. Once you decide which variety of fraud you will search for, you then have a better idea of what, where, and how to perform the examination and what sort of clues to look for. Whatever type of fraud you choose to look for, doing so will require unique methods, perhaps expert assistance, a special place to look for the chosen fraud, and a special time to look. If you decide to search for defective delivery fraud, you may choose to forgo a detailed examination of any documents and go directly to the item that was allegedly delivered. If it was delivered in accordance with the purchase order or contract specifications, examination of those records may be all that is necessary to accomplish the audit program objectives. If the item that was allegedly delivered requires a technical determination of adequacy, investigators will have to acquire whatever technical assistance may be necessary to make that determination. They may engage a technical specialist to assist them, or provide samples of the product delivered for laboratory analysis. Also, they may choose to examine transactions that took place only during a certain time period, such as at the end of a fiscal year, when bogus transactions are more likely to occur and organizational units may have authority to spend their excess budget. Alternatively, they may choose to select their samples from the period immediately subsequent to their last audit.

SELECTING A FRAUD TYPE

Selecting the type of fraud that will be the object of your search can be relatively simple or relatively involved. It can be arbitrary and decided literally by the toss of a coin on the spur of the moment. However, more experienced people carefully schedule fraud types to be investigated a year or more in advance, to ensure that ultimately they address all fraud types they wish to visit. Because you cannot look for everything, you must choose what type of fraud to look for at any given time. Whatever type of fraud you choose to search for, you must keep in mind that the procedures employed to detect it will likely miss another fraud type that may be thriving. However, to minimize the possibility of missing a fraud type completely, over a set time period investigators attempt to include a mix of all fraud types to which the entity is vulnerable. They also usually consider preparing a proactive schedule taking into account the entity's prior experience with fraud, either suspected or proven. If the entity has had prior cases of suspected fraud, that fraud category should be given higher priority in the annual program. For example, if the entity has had a disturbing experience with duplicate payments to vendors or contractors, that fraud type should definitely be included in the upcoming schedule.

FRAUD INVESTIGATION PROCEDURE

The following is the basic procedure that should be followed in performing a proactive—and subsequently reactive—fraud-specific review. For demonstration purposes, the example case is hypothetical and extremely simple. Nevertheless, the basic procedure is essentially the same for more involved and higher-dollar-value cases.

Decide Which Type of Fraud to Search For

Let us assume you choose to search for multiple payee fraud, which involves paying a legitimate vendor's invoice two or more times but issuing the additional checks to different payees. Usually, each fictitious payee name chosen is different in order to preclude the accidental detection of duplicate payments to the same payee.

Select a Suitable Accounting Transaction

Select a suitable accounting transaction that has been paid sometime within the past year that distinguishes the fraud type selected. Obtain relevant underlying document records and files for the transaction selected and become familiar with contract or purchase order terms and product or service requirements, as may be appropriate. No verifications need to be done at this point in the examination.

Perform the Investigative Procedures

Multiple payee fraud is similar to duplicate payment fraud but is several degrees harder to detect. In duplicate payment fraud, the basic detection process involves scanning the payments made to a single vendor and identifying payments of like amounts for further examination. Any duplicates that are detected will be either unintentional errors (which do happen from time to time) or possibly fraud. In seeking to detect multiple payee fraud, scanning a single vendor's account for identical payment amounts will not reveal the fraudulent payments being sought. The perpetrator will have selected different payees as the recipients of record for whatever product or service justified the payment(s) so that accidental discovery is less likely. Multiple payee fraud is the fraud of choice for many perpetrators because it is relatively simple to conduct and it is not as easy to detect as duplicate payment fraud.

Perpetrators find multiple payee fraud convenient in that all of the justification underlying a payment to legitimate Contractor A—including a satisfactory receiving report—may be used to justify an identical payment to Contractor B and possibly Contractors C, D, and E. For example, inexperienced investigators who might select the payment to Contractor B for examination would not be likely to dwell on it because a legitimate project is involved, and it would be found to be properly authorized and satisfactorily delivered. What else is there to determine? However, the legitimate purchase order or contract could have been easily changed to Contractor B's name (or a similar but fabricated name) and a phony invoice prepared.

Multiple payee fraud is likely to be detected only if you are looking for it. If so, you will know that a limited examination of underlying documents will not disclose the fraud, nor will an inspection of the actual work or goods delivered. Accordingly, some people will limit or omit critical examination of the documents. They may visit the worksite, if it is a construction project, not to inspect the work but to attempt to elicit information from employees who witnessed the work being done, asking "Who did the work?" If it were goods or a service that was delivered, the same tactic may be useful. The questions "Who was the distributor?" or "Who was the service provider?" would be asked of possible witnesses.

An advisory note is appropriate here. You must never underestimate the cunning of fraud perpetrators even though some of them do turn out to be inept. Truly clever perpetrators will be aware of methods to detect their activities and will not select dissimilar names for the fictitious payees. Rather, they will be more likely to select phonetically similar names, such as the Smith Company versus the Smyth Company, or to make an insignificant character transposition in the multiple payee names so that it seems as if typographical error was made. They do this to throw off investigators. If someone tells an investigator that the Smith Company did the work, it could easily be inferred that the Smyth Company was the contractor or vendor. It is also done to circumvent computer analysis that displays all the work performed by only the Smith Company. Any names that are not spelled S-m-i-t-h will not be displayed.

If no indicia of fraud are discovered, you must decide whether to pass the transaction selected—because time is valuable—or to go on. The decision is up to you, and you may do either. However, if you were to pass this particular transaction, you would have missed an opportunity to discover fraud.

Many people neglect to utilize the power of computer databases for verification. For example, if a transaction represents payment for a maintenance or repair project, it is very likely that any expenditures will be posted to recurring maintenance project ledgers. The entity's building maintenance department may maintain a record of the maintenance performed on each building—how many times and when a building or its rooms were painted, for example, or when the roof was resurfaced and when the floors were recarpeted. These sorts of data are essential for planning purposes. Because these nonaccounting records very likely are posted from invoices paid, any multiple payments would probably show up as duplicate postings to these records. If the multiple payments were for inventory items, then quite possibly, a review of inventory control records would reveal the duplicate postings. In fact, you may well consider initiating checking of multiple payee fraud from records of item shortages disclosed by physical inventory counts. Obviously, if a multiple payee fraud involves paying two or more times for the purchase of a single item of inventory, a subsequent physical inventory count will reveal a shortage.

If Indicia Are Not Found

If no indicia of fraud are discovered, investigators will pass the transaction and go on to another selection.

If Indicia Are Found

If indicia of fraud are found, the investigator must seek additional evidence to validate the finding. For illustration purposes, assume that the transaction selected involved a payment of $25,000 to the Smith Company to resurface employee parking lot number 3. On inquiring further, it was discovered that the Jones Company may have performed the work, and a review of payments to the Jones Company discovered a paid invoice for $25,000 for resurfacing employee parking lot number 3. Furthermore, a visit to the address given for the Smith Company uncovers an empty lot.

In cases such as this when strong evidence of fraud is discovered, you must take extra care to assure that the findings remain confidential, and begin to discreetly search for additional instances of the same fraud. Although the evidence given in the illustration is strong enough to indicate that fraud has occurred, if prosecution is to be considered, it would be advisable to attempt to detect corroborating evidence. With just one case in evidence, the perpetrator(s), particularly if they are first-time offenders, are not likely to be convicted in a lenient court, or they may be convicted but given a lenient sentence. However, experience has shown that when perpetrators are successful and are not detected, they will attempt other similar frauds and often will not change their successful modus operandi. That is, there is a good chance that, in this case, the Smith Company will again be the bogus recipient of multiple payments. Accordingly, continuing examinations should begin with a search for any and all payments to the Smith Company. If any are found, they should be investigated. Note: One reason that perpetrators are likely to keep using the Smith Company is that they may have established a bank account under that name, and it is convenient to clear all checks through it. Other transactions involving the suspect(s) should be examined for similar bogus payments or other frauds, under the theory that once auditors have found a thief, other thefts are likely. Consider once again the fishing analogy. Once a fisherman has identified a fishing hole and caught a fish, he will fish the hole repeatedly in the expectation that he may have found the mother lode.

The initial finding of the fraudulent Smith Company should be discussed with the audit committee, if there is one, or whichever other company official has been designated as the confidante. Every chief auditor should have one. If there is no audit committee, usually the controller or chief financial officer is designated. During this meeting, you should discuss the engagement of an investigator to pursue case development. The investigator should be brought into case development after the danger of any premature publicity is minimized. The investigator should be provided with any evidence that was uncovered during the examination. After he or she has finished work, the case will be reviewed by council and a decision whether to prosecute will be made.

When prosecution is considered seriously, a prosecutor should be contacted. All fraud cases in which the sum of evidence is sufficient to eliminate reasonable doubt should be prosecuted. The company should also notify its fidelity bond carrier that it has discovered a possible fraud and that an investigation is underway.

CASE 5.1   The Phantom Renovations

The internal auditor once attempted to verify approximately $450,000 in renovations and other improvements made to an older medical clinic building. Were he the typical internal auditor, he probably would have examined the underlying documents and found them all to be in order and all properly signed by medical administrators, including attestations that the improvements had been delivered satisfactorily. The average internal auditor would have taken no exceptions to the $450,000 project. However, he was an exceptionally good auditor and chose to visit the site of the improvements to see them for himself. When he went to inspect the work that had been done, he found that the building had been demolished and a new building stood in its place.

Astounded, he reasoned, "Why would anyone spend

$450,000 in improvements to an old building that was soon to be demolished?" Of course, he suspected fraud. However, he was at a dead end as far as the fraud evidence was concerned.

What would be your reaction were you to discover these circumstances? How do you verify that the $450,000 in improvements claimed were actually made? Sounds very suspicious. Ways and means of verifying delivery of the improvements were considered, as was the engagement of a private investigator. The auditor planned to begin interviewing the various people who may have had knowledge of the improvements, including contractors, workers, medical clinic employees, and so forth. He suspected that clinic administrators attempted to cover a $450,000 unexplainable loss, very probably fraud, by charging it to the old clinic building, knowing it would be torn down within six months. The question to be answered was: "What explanation would the contractors give when asked what they delivered for the $450,000 paid?" Because of the blatant nature of the circumstances, it is quite possible that medical management in this case did not want the $450,000 expenditure investigated and the auditor who was involved may have been told to "forget it." Auditors sometimes are faced with this sort of dilemma and must decide how to react. They have the hard choice of either "forgetting about it" and becoming part of a cover-up, or pursuing it and being fired.

SUMMARY

In carrying out a fraud investigation plan, you must be resourceful and know that all examinations will not be as successful as the case described. However, you will seldom be bored. In keeping with the old adage that "If something can possibly go wrong, it will!"

NOTES

1. Agatha Christie, mystery writer, 1890–1976.
2. Anonymous; http://www.quotegarden.com/fishing.html.
3. Henry David Thoreau, author, poet, and philosopher, 1817–1862; http://www.brainyquote.com/quotes/quotes/h/henrydavid107147.html.
4. Steven Wright, comedian, 1955– ; http://www.quotationspage.com/quote/1244.html.

6

ELEMENTARY FRAUD TYPES

While we are talking about elementary types of fraud, perhaps we can set the record straight on a literary note. Although the phrase, "Elementary, my dear Watson" is often attributed to Sherlock Holmes, the British detective in the works of Sir Arthur Conan Doyle, Holmes never actually said it in any of the written works. Holmes is supposed to have uttered the phrase to his amazed companion, Dr. Watson, as he explained his reasoning in solving a crime. These precise words are never used in the Holmes stories; however, a similar phrase appears in the story "The Crooked Man": "Excellent!' I [Watson] cried. 'Elementary,' said he."

THREE ELEMENTARY FRAUD TYPES: DEFINITIONS

This chapter begins the fraud investigation practice segment of the text with three elementary fraud types. They are rather simple to understand and are immensely popular with perpetrators who have limited opportunities to commit fraud; hence, fraud investigators cannot ignore testing for them periodically. This chapter defines and discusses three fraud types: duplicate payment fraud, multiple payee fraud, and shell fraud.

Perpetration of the three types is relatively simple, which is perhaps why these frauds are practiced so widely. Many entities inadvertently make duplicate payments that are detected only when honest creditors return the duplicate checks. Although these three fraud types are relatively simple to commit, they are not always equally simple to detect, and all require very different detection methods to reveal them. However using the appropriate detection procedures, on a comparative scale, all are among the easiest of frauds to detect. In the sections that follow, each fraud type is discussed further and includes a discussion of the various detection techniques and difficulties therein. Bear in mind that each fraud type requires different detection methods. For that reason, you should decide which type of fraud you are going to search for before you begin.

Duplicate Payment Fraud

As the name implies, duplicate payment fraud involves the issue of two or more identical checks to pay the same debt. One serves to pay the creditor, while the other(s) are recovered and cashed by the perpetrator.

Normally the fraud occurs when an employee of an entity, with criminal intent, initiates the necessary documentation to cause an additional payment(s) to be made to a vendor or contractor to satisfy a debt. The employee may act alone or in collusion with an employee of the vendor or contractor. The perpetrator arranges to intercept the second check, and any additional checks that may be issued, and cash them.

Multiple Payee Fraud

Multiple payee fraud is similar to duplicate payment fraud with a most important difference—the payment checks are not identical. This fraud involves two or more payments to different vendors or contractors for the same debt. One of the payees usually is the one that actually delivered the product or services. The other(s) is either fraudulent or a conspirator in the fraud. The fraud probably was invented by someone familiar with fraud detection methods, in that multiple payee fraud is not detected as easily as duplicate payment fraud.

Shell Fraud

Shell fraud involves payments to vendors or contractors—real or fictitious—in payment of alleged debts for fictitious projects, materials, or services. All underlying documentation is forged. It may or may not involve conspiracy with contractors or suppliers. All of the payment money generated is pocketed by the perpetrator(s).

DUPLICATE PAYMENT FRAUD

Almost every company has had the experience of unintentionally paying an invoice twice during the rush of business. It can happen very easily. Sometimes when payment is delayed, the vendor or contractor sends a second invoice, and both get paid. Note: companies should not be paying vendors based on receipt of a statement; they should only pay on an original invoice. When duplicate payments do occur, they usually happen very innocently on the part of all parties involved. Most times duplicate payments are returned by the recipients or credited to the paying entity's account.

However, when fraud is involved, an employee of the paying entity normally initiates whatever procedures are required to cause one or more checks to be issued that are identical to a check that already has been issued in payment of a legitimate debt. The duplicate payment(s) is intercepted or otherwise acquired by the perpetrator. If the paying entity's internal controls are weak, the perpetrator simply takes the check out of the outgoing mail. Sometimes the perpetrator will telephone the payee and explain that a duplicate check was inadvertently sent and that he/she would appreciate it if it would be returned. The fact that the payee's name is indicated on the check is usually no problem for a clever perpetrator. For example, a taxpayer's check made out to the IRS was actually stolen out of the IRS's mail and altered to read I R Stevenson!

The employee/perpetrator may initiate the duplicate payment using a second copy of the vendor's invoice, which is easy to get simply by asking for one, or by simply photocopying or scanning the original invoice. Copiers and scanners may be used to reproduce any number of copies of an invoice—in faithful color—with little difficulty. Purchase orders, receiving documents, and the like prepared for the original invoice may be copied in order to "document" the duplicate payments. All approval signatures and initials can be forged. Internal controls may or may not be a deterrent.

Sometimes a dishonest employee will conspire with a vendor's employee, in which case the conspirator will provide second invoices, simplifying the preparation of a second check in payment, and assure acquisition of the duplicate payment check. If due care is taken in perpetrating duplicate payment fraud, the duplicate payment is rarely noticed, provided the perpetrating employee is not particularly greedy or careless.

Unless internal auditors or other investigators are specifically looking for duplicate payment fraud, it is unlikely that it will be detected. Each of the duplicate payments is a complete and separate transaction, and each documentation package is complete and authentic, without flaws, and ordinarily will survive audit testing not designed to look for duplicate payments. If any one of the payments is selected for examination—either the original or one of the duplicates—traditional auditing practices will find the documentation package to be in perfect order. If auditors attempt to verify the product or service involved, they will find it was fully delivered with no exceptions to be taken. Unless they accidentally happen to select both payments for transaction testing, an extremely unlikely event, neither transaction will be likely to attract traditional auditors' attention. In addition, audit testing performed to discover any of the other elementary frauds discussed in this chapter will not discover duplicate payment fraud.

However, if investigators have chosen to search for duplicate payment fraud, it is relatively easy to discover. Investigators look for identical payment amounts made to the same payee. Their scan of payment amounts can be done manually, for small businesses, visually using a computer, or by using an automated search program, which utilizes data mining software to display identical payment amounts made to the same payees.[1] If the documents bear identical dates, product items, and other characteristics, auditors can usually assume they are duplicates. Most businesses or companies that discover duplicate payments automatically assume that error was involved. However, that can soon change when the payee insists that it received only one payment. A payee acknowledging that it received two payments generally—but not necessarily—indicates that the payment was not fraudulent. Some vendors, or more likely one of their employees, have been known to conspire in this type of fraud.

Before or after contacting the payee, auditors who suspect a duplicate payment also may verify the apparent duplicate receipt (or non-receipt) of goods or services by consulting information system records such as inventory, maintenance or housekeeping records, and the like, which usually are used to record the receipt of goods or services. A physical inspection of the items or services purchased is useful only if it is possible to inspect both apparent purchases. If any discrepancy is discovered, it is probably advisable to expand the verification procedure. Sometimes common sense alone will tell auditors that it is unlikely that two of a unique product, such as two roofs, were installed on warehouse number 3 during the same time period.

A word of advice to auditors—be as cunning as the perpetrator is likely to be. If perpetrators are intelligent and aware of your discovery methods, they will make adjustments to frustrate your search. If they make the slightest change in a duplicate payment amount—as little as one cent in applying a cash discount, for example—a computer matching of payment amounts will fail. The search will not yield $12,397.14 as a duplicate of $12,397.13. To a computer, they are two different numbers.

MULTIPLE PAYEE FRAUD

Multiple payee fraud involves two or more payments to different payees for the same item or service. One of the payments will be to the legitimate creditor; the other payment(s) will be fraudulent.

Perpetration of multiple payee fraud is relatively easy in that, as in duplicate payment fraud, most of the supporting documentation underlying the legitimate transaction can be switched to support the bogus transaction(s) and will serve to give the bogus transaction(s) the appearance of legitimacy. Supporting documentation for the bogus payments usually utilizes the same purchase authorizations, purchase orders, and receiving reports as were used for the legitimate transaction. Most will allow the bogus transactions to pass all but the most exacting of examinations including confirmation with entity requesting or ordering officials.

The multiple payee fraud perpetrators may work alone. A bogus vendor name may be used, with an address or post office box controlled by the perpetrator to receive all payments. Multiple payee fraud is relatively detection resistant if the employee/perpetrator works in collusion with an employee of an existing vendor. In such cases, fraudsters can use legitimate invoices and mailing addresses.

Multiple payee fraud is not difficult to discover—if it is being looked for—but it is more difficult to detect than duplicate payment fraud. If traditional auditors were to, by chance, select a transaction involving multiple payee fraud for examination, the transaction undoubtedly would pass most customary audit tests without any exceptions taken. Either of the duplicate payment files would have a fully documented support file that would satisfy most auditors. Also, audit procedures designed to detect duplicate payment frauds would not detect multiple payee fraud because no one vendor listing would have more than one of the payments on it, so scanning would not disclose any exceptions. If either payment is compared to the product or service that is being paid for, no exceptions are likely to be noticed.

Perhaps the quickest and easiest way, although not the surest, for auditors to search for multiple payee payments is to:

1. Select payments of goods or services to verify.
2. Visit the site so that the project, goods, or services can be examined.

At the site, you can inspect the items in question in an attempt to determine if the performing contractor or vendor signed or marked the item delivered in any way. Many contractors do sign their work, and vendors usually mark the cartons delivered. If you can determine who delivered the items in this manner, and can match it to the payee selected, the test is over. Of course, you may be unlucky enough to select the payment that was made to the actual performing contractor or vendor, and miss the bogus payment.

However, if it appears that a contractor or vendor other than the one whose name appears on the payment voucher actually delivered the item, you may have found evidence of multiple payee fraud, where two or more contractors were paid for one service, product, or project delivered. The finding should be considered indicia of fraud, and you must check it out. To do so, it will be necessary to go back to the disbursement or contracting files and attempt to find the payment made to the new contractor or vendor name identified with the project, goods, or service examined. If you can locate the payment made to the contractor or vendor who it appears actually delivered the item in question, you may have proven at least one example of multiple payee fraud.

If you cannot find the delivering vendor or contractor's mark on the item inspected, inquiries should be made of persons who might know who supplied the product or services. This may be investigation by conversation, but it is acceptable if it accomplishes the purpose. For example, if it is a construction job, when you visit the construction site, discuss the project with employees who may have observed the work when it was being done. Of course, the line of questioning need not convey the conversation's real purpose. You might begin a conversation with people in the area, and innocently remark, "Nice work. Do you know who did it?" If it involves services delivered, the same conversation is usually effective if the person you speak with is aware of whom the contractor is. There is a caveat; discretion is essential. You should not be so overt as to make it obvious that fraud is suspected.

> *Think like a wise man but communicate in the language of the people.*[2]

Queries frequently bring out the name of the real contractor who performed the work, with a remark such as "Yeah, the Charlie Company knows what they're doing." Not exactly high-tech, but it can be effective. If supplies are involved, you can visit the storage area and examine the supply boxes. Often the packages bear the supplier's name or advertising. If the source names agree with the name on the payment document being examined, you may consider dropping the item and moving on to another. If the payment has been made to Delta Company, and it appears that Charlie Company shipped the goods, you may have indicia of fraud that must be resolved. If suspicions of multiple payment fraud are strong enough, you must begin a search for the other payees, one of whom will be the vendor or contractor who actually delivered the product.

Depending on the accounting and information systems in use, other verification options may be available. Where multiple payments may be a possibility, they are likely to bear the same accounting codes. For example, if an item selected for examination bears an accounting code 2100 (which, let us assume, is the code for exterior maintenance) a scan of accounting code 2100 items may limit the transactions that will have to be reviewed. For example, you can retrieve and display all account 2100 transactions for the 90-day period surrounding the date of the transaction being examined, or perhaps the number of transactions may not be too excessive to scan all of them visually for similarities of amounts, or even the names of suppliers or contractors.

Additional testing to detect multiple payee fraud depends on the reliability of the systems in use by the possible victim. In all proactive fraud examinations, you should be reasonably familiar with all nonaccounting information systems available and know how they can be used to reveal information that the accounting records do not. For example, if the entity being examined maintains logs of maintenance performed on plant buildings or maintains a record of painting, which many entities do, a review of the records may reveal that the building involved was painted twice in a short span of time. A review of these records may indicate a suspicious level or frequency of work performed, which can lead to a review of applicable payments. It is also possible that if a bogus painting contract was selected accidentally, by cross-checking it to the information system you might find that the painting was never posted to the painting record—an omission that should be questioned.

Why not scan the payments register for identical payments to discover multiple payee fraud? If a new warehouse roof was installed for $75,000, wouldn't detection result if $75,000 payments were scanned? Not if the perpetrator was at least moderately clever. First, remember that unlike duplicate payment fraud, payee names will be different, so any scanning would have to be with regard to amounts only. Further, there is nothing to prevent the perpetrator of multiple payee fraud from varying the amount of the payment. One of the new roof payments might be $75,000 and the other could be $71,500.

SHELL FRAUD

Shell fraud probably got its name from the old carnival game where con artists very obviously place an object under one of three half shells, each of which resembled half of a tennis ball. They would then rapidly move the shells around in such a manner that the victim was always certain that the object was under one of the shells and was always sure where it was. The victim then would bet a sum of money that he or she was right. Of course, the con artists were experts at making the object disappear, so that it was not under any of the shells. No matter which shell the victim selected, it would be the wrong one. Shell frauds are so called because, like the object under the shells, the item that was purchased and paid for did not exist and never existed. The basis for shell fraud payments is totally fictitious.

Be not ashamed of mistakes and thus make them crimes.[3]

In executing shell fraud, the perpetrator conceives of a fictional purchase and prepares paperwork and accounting entries, forging whatever signatures are necessary to acquire an item or service. Paperwork might include requisitions, purchase orders or contracts, and receiving reports—indeed, whatever is needed to complete the document files. They are all forged and fictitious. Finally, all the perpetrator must do to obtain payment is submit a simple bogus invoice at the proper time. Depending on the size of the entity and the internal controls in place, a perpetrator can work alone to accomplish a shell fraud, particularly if he or she is in a key position. Normally, however, shell frauds are best accomplished using an actual vendor or contractor serving in a conspiratorial role.

The federal government has experienced many cases of shell fraud. One case was previously mentioned in Chapter 4 (Case 4.1). It involved the government's office supply stores operating in various cities throughout the country, for the convenience of government agencies. It is useful to amplify some of the facts of this case for purposes of this chapter. Supply store managers were given the authority to purchase various items from commercial sources in wholesale quantities and to resell them to government customers on a retail basis. As previously noted, the government agency received a note from a jilted girlfriend of a store manager telling of his fraudulent practices. Subsequent audit and investigation initially discovered that, in one store, brokers wholesaling various products were conspiring with store managers to purchase office supply products without any intention to deliver them or for the store to sell them.

All that was necessary was for the store manager to prepare a purchase order to buy $5,000 worth of ball-point pens through the broker. Two or three weeks later, the store manager would prepare a receiving report to confirm that the pens had been received, even though they had not. A short time later, the broker mailed an invoice to the servicing government finance office. With the purchase order, the receiving report, and the vendor's invoice in hand, the automated payment system would mail a $5,000 check to the invoice address. At no time were the pens shipped. The cost was absorbed by charging higher prices on other merchandise sold. Because the stores, at that time, were operating on the retail inventory method of accounting, control of the fraudulent practice was difficult. Because it was impossible to determine what individual inventory item levels should be at any given time, it was not possible to take physical inventory counts and compare them to book inventory levels to detect shortages. Subsequently, automated item bar coding was implemented for inventory control and sales, making the fraud much more difficult to perpetrate.

Many other instances of shell fraud also have been disclosed. Building maintenance projects seem to be a target of choice among perpetrators. There have been paint jobs that were never done, walls that were never constructed to divide large rooms and buildings that were never built. However, all were well documented with forged papers and bogus computer entries, and all fictitious vendors were paid promptly. In another instance, the testing of an agency's automated supply control system detected what was believed to be an internal control weakness that would have permitted shell fraud. Testing it, utilizing a remote computer, the investigators were able to enter an electronic purchase order into the system for $98,000 in tool kits, with an imaginary tool kit distributor. After delaying for about three weeks to give the imaginary distributor time to "deliver" the tool kits, the investigators used the same computer to "advise" the inventory control system that the tool kits had been received in the warehouse. The investigators then mailed a custom-printed invoice to the agency billing them $98,000, allowing a 2 percent cash discount for prompt payment. Within two weeks the investigators had a check in their hands for about $96,000. The cash discount had helped speed payment.

The best way to obtain assurance that shell fraud has not occurred is to determine that the project, supplies, or service has been delivered as claimed, at or about the time claimed, if at all possible. It simply involves selecting a payment transaction, selecting one or more line items from it, and going wherever it is necessary to verify that the item has, in fact, been delivered. Reviewing maintenance records will not work.

To illustrate that shell frauds can be dollar significant, in another case a perpetrator submitted totally fictitious purchase orders, receiving reports, and invoices for building cleaning services that were never performed. The services were for things such as carpet cleaning, washing walls, and cleaning blinds, and each invoice averaged about $10,000. The total aggregate fraud committed in this manner over several years was over $900,000. Luckily, the fraud was discovered accidentally. If the accidental discovery had not occurred, the fraud may never have been disclosed through auditing unless the internal auditor had the exceptional good fortune to select one of the perpetrator's invoices for fictional services soon after the service had been delivered and found that the carpet or the blinds had not been cleaned.

It is difficult to verify nondelivery in this type of shell fraud once too much time has passed. Also, where a consumable commodity has been purchased or a service is involved, it is not possible to see, touch, or feel it to confirm its delivery. In many instances, it is not reasonably possible to inspect the work allegedly done.

Consider the difficulty in verifying that a dedicated electrical service line has been installed once a wall covering has been installed over it. The question always is how to verify that the service was delivered. The more ingenious the investigator, the more successful he or she will be in finding fraud.

There is no easy way to determine whether various products, projects, services, or supplies have been delivered when they cannot be readily identified and inspected. And, of course, clever perpetrators can be expected to target this sort of opportunity to commit fraud because verification is a bit more difficult. When inspection is not possible, fraud investigators must attempt to verify that the items were delivered by contacting the supplier or contractor. This, of course, assumes that the suppliers or contractors are not in a criminal conspiracy with the internal perpetrator. But you must—at first, at least—trust that there is no conspiracy and talk to the other party. If that person says that no such job was performed, you are lucky. In many cases there will not be a conspiracy, and the supplier or contractor will quickly deny that anything was delivered.

When contacting the supplier or contractor, you should not raise suspicions that anything improper is suspected. Rather, you can ask circuitous questions that verify the project was delivered, such as: "We are reviewing the X Company's relationship with its suppliers. Were you paid on a timely basis for project X?"

Also, internal records-receiving registers, receiving documents, or even personnel records, which will vary from entity to entity, may offer avenues for verification. You must become acquainted with them. For example, if Henry Jones signed for the receipt of the delivery of a large project, ask: "Was Henry Jones on duty the day the receipt was signed?" You must be imaginative and creative. Once, when I was faced with an obvious perpetrator who denied vehemently that he had anything to do with an internal fraud, I analyzed 6 years' worth of personnel records, only to find that the alleged perpetrator was the only person who had worked continuously throughout the period for the company—a guilty plea ensued shortly thereafter!

Consider the following examples of shell fraud based on actual cases.

CASE 6.1   The Refurbished Water Tank

Government investigators specifically looking for shell fraud selected a $5,000 payment that had been made to a general contractor for refurbishing a 10,000-gallon water tank located atop a 10- story building. The contract called for the contractor to drain the tank, scrape and clean the interior, coat the walls with a sealant, and refill the tank with water.

Because the investigators were searching for evidence of a shell fraud, they proceeded directly to the work-site to determine if the work had been accomplished. At the investigators' request, the building manager, who had signed the receiving report attesting that the work had been done, showed them the tank high atop the building. He laughed, saying they would have a hard time inspecting the work, for the tank was full of water. But the investigators, who were experienced in fraud detection, anticipated the problem and had engaged the assistance of a technician who was qualified to inspect the work.

The technician rode the elevator to the building's roof and climbed the steel ladder attached to the side of the tank. At the top, he swung the access hatch aside, rolled up his sleeve, reached into the tank, and felt the interior surface. Next, he dragged his hand up along the side of the tank and withdrew it from the water. He held a handful of rusty scale proving that the tank had never been refurbished. This may seem like a simple conclusion, but many companies and their auditors have been duped over the years by not employing somewhat elementary technical assistance. Don't be a hero—have others help when necessary.

We can't all be heroes because somebody has to sit on the curb
and clap as they go by.[4]

CASE 6.2   The Phantom Building Services

In an organization responsible for the management and maintenance of buildings in six states, an accounting clerk with access to the financial plans of all the buildings systematically
forged the necessary documents to cause payments for building cleaning services that were never received. For example,
he would prepare a purchase order requesting a cleaning service and forge a building manager's name. The document
would be duly recorded in the accounting system as a purchase in process. The clerk used a fictitious contractor's name
and a post office box address, which he controlled. Two or
three weeks later, the clerk would forge a receiving report to
advise the system that the service had been performed. Shortly
thereafter, he would mail an invoice for between $10,000 and
$20,000. The system, noting that all prerequisites for payment
had been satisfied, would mail a check to his post office box.
He was eventually caught, accidentally, and prosecuted for
perpetrating $300,000 in fraud. Privately, the auditors esti-
mated his total theft was closer to $900,000.

Analysis

A likely discovery strategy: This was a shell fraud that was
discovered accidentally when a cash-short building manager,
operating during a period of corporate austerity and facing
budget cutbacks, was challenged for performing discretionary
maintenance at a time when he was seeking additional budget
authority for necessary maintenance. In better times, the
fraud may not have been discovered. However, in this case,

had an auditor happened to select one of the many fraudulent cleaning payments and asked the building manager if the cleaning service was performed, he would have said no. Of course, if the building manager had been the perpetrator, he would have said yes. Actually, the building manager was among the prime suspects, and direct questions of that sort were not considered.

In this case, as in many similar cases, the perpetrator used a fictitious contractor's name in submitting building services invoices. However, had one of the bogus invoices been selected for testing, a simple test—that is, determining if the contractor was legitimate—would have disclosed the fraud. Reference to telephone directories, Dun & Bradstreet credit directories, an Internet search for any listings, and similar business reference directories could have provided the clue that the payees were fictitious.

In fact, many companies are now having a credit manager run these checks before a vendor is accepted into the system and to verify existence of such a vendor.

Where usual sources do not confirm the existence of a vendor, a resourceful employee will find another way. In one instance, where a clerk became suspicious of a machine parts supplier allegedly located in a distant city, the clerk called a friend located in that city and asked them to drive by the address. No surprise—they found an empty lot!

Whoever is detected in a shameful fraud is ever after not believed even if they speak the truth.[5]

NOTES

1. A search of the Internet using "data mining software" as key words will direct the reader to many choices for such items.

2. William Butler Yeats, Irish poet, 1865–1939; http://www.quotationspage .com/quote/2396.html.

3. Confucius, 551 BCE, 459 BCE; http://www.quotationspage.com/quotes /Confucius/.

4. Will Rogers, humorist and showman, 1879-1935; http://www.quotationspage .com/quote/673.html.

5. Phaedrus, Macedonian inventor and writer, 15 BCE–50 CE; http://www .giga-usa.com/gigaweb1/quotes2/quautphaedrusx001.htm.

7

FRAUD DEFECTIVES

DEFECTIVE DELIVERY FRAUD

Defective delivery fraud involves the delivery of products or services that are inferior in some manner. Further, the vendor or contractor (1) intentionally causes the delivery to be defective; (2) does not disclose the defect to the customer, and (3) does not offer a corresponding decrease in price to compensate the customer for the defective products or services. The products delivered may be short in quantity and/or of inferior quality to that ordered and paid for. This type of fraud occurs very frequently and should be a regular proactive fraud target.

Defective delivery fraud involves the secret substitution of cheaper (lower quality) material, lower quantities of materials, cheaper (less skilled) labor, and/or fewer labor hours than the buying entity bargained for, without disclosing the substitution to the contracting entity and without giving a corresponding reduction in price. The perpetrating contractor or supplier profits to the extent of the reductions or substitutions that have been made. As an example, defective delivery fraud might involve a building contractor who cheats on the sand and cement mixture used in constructing bridges and buildings. The resulting concrete eventually crumbles and the bridge or building collapses.

All proactive fraud-specific examinations periodically should include procedures designed to detect defective delivery fraud, which occurs in several variations. This chapter is dedicated to communicating a comprehensive understanding of this fraud type and illustrating some of its many variations.

Many times, a conspiracy between the contractor or vendor and a key employee of the victim is necessary for defective receipt fraud to work. That is, normally a vendor or contractor considering defective delivery fraud would be deterred by a competent, loyal employee of the victim, who would be charged with determining whether delivery met the employer's requirements. If the victim's employee is dishonest and in collusion with the delivering vendor, then the delivering vendor has nothing to fear—unless, of course, someone is proactively looking for defective delivery fraud. Of course, it should be noted that ultimately, if a building or structure fails because of inferior materials (charged at a higher level), an investigation will ensue and the perpetrators are likely to be found.

An inattentive or distracted employee will not notice the fraud being perpetrated on the company. The risk of this situation being a factor in a company is dependent upon the working environment of the employees. As with many types of fraud, if purchasing department or contracts department employees are overworked, underpaid, dissatisfied with work, or are just "receiving a paycheck," the likelihood of a defective delivery fraud without employee collusion can increase. In these cases, the fraudulent vendor or contractor will try to "sneak" one by the receiving employee and will claim an "honest mistake" in the paperwork if caught. Experience has shown that most frauds start out small, effectively "testing the waters," and that once internal controls can be breached by small frauds without detection, larger ones are bound to follow.

Most internal control systems require that designated employees must complete a receiving report or other attestation certifying that the product or service was delivered in accordance with applicable purchase order or contract specifications before a vendor's invoice is processed for payment. However, if the employee responsible for accepting the delivery is noticeably negligent and easily distracted in performing this responsibility, a vendor or contractor may exploit this. Sometimes vendors or contractors are known to be generous with gifts to customers' key employees or to lavishly entertain them. The payback to the vendor is often only a perfunctory examination of incoming goods or services received from those contractors. The amount, type, and size of gifts to a purchasing agent can be very telling about the relationship they have with their customers and a potential red flag for the company to take notice.

Gifts Can Play a Part in Defective Delivery Fraud

One would hope that most companies would have a written policy on receipt of gifts, entertainment, and the like. Most companies in this day and age choose to prohibit any type of gifts or entertainment received by anyone in any position that might be influenced by a service provider or vendor. One of the most impressive publicly available statements is that made by Brunswick Corporation. Under the ethics page of their web site, the following can be found:

> The Company operates in many nations around the world, and we trust our employees to use their best judgment when it comes to business gifts, favors or entertainment. In the United States, as in other nations, at times it may be respectful and appropriate to offer or receive business gifts, favors or entertainment—but never to any U.S. or foreign governmental official. Additionally, all of us must remember to represent the highest standards of integrity and fairness in our daily decisions. As such, bribes and other forms of payments that are designed to improperly influence others are never acceptable.
>
> As a gesture of mutual appreciation and gratitude, the Company allows employees to offer or receive business gifts, favors and entertainment within specific guidelines. Such gifts should never include cash and should never cause you to make a decision you would not have made otherwise. Attending or participating in

a Company-sponsored event, such as a dinner or golf outing, is not a gift.

As an employee, you should not make, nor participate in making, any payments designed to cause or improperly influence an individual, a company or a governmental official to act in a way that gives the Company or yourself an advantage. In addition, you cannot solicit, encourage or actually receive any bribe or other payment, contribution, gift or favor which could influence your decision. Because the circumstances aren't always clear, when in doubt you should consult with your supervisor, Ethics Counselor, Division Legal Department or other appropriate contact.

What is it?

A bribe or improper payment is designed to influence another's behavior and is always prohibited. A bribe could take the form of direct cash payments or other forms of payment, such as:

- Kickbacks,
- Unexplained rebates,
- Advertising or other disguised allowances, or
- Invoices for advertising or some other disguised expense.

Acceptable business gifts, favors or entertainment comply with the Guide under the following guidelines:

- Are infrequent and not excessive in value (defined as $200 or a lower amount set by your Division);
- Comply with U.S. laws and local laws in foreign countries;
- Would not embarrass the Company, the person receiving the gift or the person giving the gift; and
- Are never given to, or received from, any U.S. or foreign governmental official.

The Company requires employees to disclose, in writing, any business gift, favor or entertainment, other than business meals, given or received, that has a value of more than $200 (or a lower amount set by your Division) on a gift reporting form available from your Human Resource Department or through Lotus Notes, where available.

This form must be completed each time you give or receive a gift, other than business meals, that exceeds $200, or a lower amount set by your Division.[1]

Brunswick also gives case examples explaining what is and what is not a bribe, kickback, and so forth. With the new corporate governance regulations, public companies (and indeed many private companies) are much more transparent than in the past, and employees know exactly where they stand.

Defects in Materials or Services

Defective delivery fraud can involve defects in materials or services. Materials delivered may be defective in quality and/or quantity. Instead of the high-quality material ordered, a cheaper material may be substituted. Instead of delivering 1,000 widgets, as were ordered and paid for, only 900 may have been delivered. Services delivered may be defective in one or more of several ways. Where the contract involves time and materials, for example, instead of 1,000 hours of service invoiced, only 900 may have been expended; and whereas the hours may have been billed as involving a senior technician's time, 300 of the hours may have been the hours of an apprentice, who earns one-third of the senior technician's wages.

To illustrate further, the following sections include examples taken from actual cases of defective delivery fraud including fraudulent:

- Services provided
- Goods or products received
- Labor, wages provided
- Building, construction performed

- Excessive or overshipment of goods
- Overpricing of goods

Defective Delivery of Services

A common example of defective delivery fraud involves interior painting. Many companies defer painting interior office space for an interval of five or more years to avoid the disruption of business that it causes. However, when painting is performed, it is common for building managers to contract for two coats of paint to be applied in order to satisfactorily cover five or more years of wear and to obtain full brilliance of any new colors applied. Of course, the application of two coats of paint requires the expenditure of more labor and paint than one coat; hence, the cost is greater than that for one coat.

The government, with its millions of square feet of office space periodically in need of redecorating, has long been a victim of this variety of fraud. Every so often a government building manager has become a willing conspirator of a dishonest contractor. On one occasion at a government building, a painter had allegedly completed a very extensive interior painting job, which required two coats for all interior wall surfaces. As was normal practice when the work was completed, he sought out the building manager to verify the satisfactory completion of his work, only to find that the manager he was accustomed to dealing with was no longer employed at that building. Nevertheless, he approached a young man who had just assumed the manager's duties and asked that he sign for satisfactory receipt of the painting. He had applied only one coat of paint but offered the new manager $5,000 in cash for his certification acknowledging that two coats of paint had been applied, stating that the $5,000 payment was the customary amount expected in these circumstances for the job completion signature. Unsure of what to do, the young man said he wanted to think about it, and needed to meet the next day. He later contacted the agency's criminal investigation office, which arranged to tape record the next day's conversation with the contractor. When the painter again offered the $5,000, he was arrested and charged with bribery.

What is especially noteworthy in this illustration of an actual crime is that the painter solicited the new building manager's signature without any concern for what was a criminal act. It was, in his mind, the customary way of doing business. He did not appear to be reticent or concerned about exposing his crime, which indicates that he likely had experience with bribing others in the past.

Ordinarily, performing a defective delivery fraud investigation such as determining if two coats of paint were in fact delivered will be a problem. Even if obviously only one coat of paint had been applied, it is your opinion against that of a skilled tradesman. The problem is particularly compelling if the examination is made months after the work is completed. A fraud investigator must be concerned with compiling adequate evidence to support possible fraud charges against a painter. Their opinion would have very little worth in a court proceeding. Merely eyeballing a newly painted wall is insufficient for alleging fraud or for claiming a refund. In fact, it would be difficult even for an expert painter to conclude with certainty that only one coat was applied when two coats were required. How then can people protect themselves in this situation?

The answer is that there is no way an investigator can verify the application of two coats of paint under normal circumstances. However, do not despair. There is a way to detect this specific fraud—with a little advance planning. One method for determining whether one or two coats of paint are applied lies within the contracting entity's internal control system. Consider, for example, the control effect if all painting contracts involving two coats of paint were to specify that the first coat must include a certain tint. It is then easy to determine at any time after the paint had been applied whether the new surface includes two coats. A simple scratch in an obscure place would show two colors. Much of the government's painting now includes the requirement that the first coat be tinted to its specification.[2] Another method would be to physically inspect the painting of each coat, letting the contractor know he must have an inspection and a sign off on each coat.

In addition, the contractor should also know that these inspections may occur at any time and someone other than the contractor must indicate that the job is done. Performing a surprise inspection (or even the threat of an inspection) can be a powerful internal control.

> *As soon as I have more power over my brush, I shall work even harder than I do now . . . it will not be long before you need not send me money any more.*[3]

Defective Delivery of Goods

It's a fact that a certain type of vendor or contractor will cheat by delivering fewer products than ordered. This is done in a variety of ways. For example, staying with the paint theme, a paint manufacturer might "short fill" the paint cans he delivers to customers. Instead of putting five gallons of paint in a can, the company may consistently put in a bit less. A dairy farmer might dilute the milk he ships to dairies by adding water. In an actual case, one company would add finely crushed black rock resembling black oil sunflower seeds to its 50-pound bags of black oil sunflower bird seeds. Birds discovered the crime. They would eat the seeds and leave the black rocks!

Defective delivery frauds are not always perpetrated by the vendors who supply the materials. Not infrequently, middlemen are responsible for defective delivery of supplies. That is, a distributor may ship a customer's entire order as specified by the customer. However, the truck drivers delivering the merchandise may deliver less than a customer's full shipment, stealing some of the cargo for themselves.

If the victim's receiving personnel are not careful in counting the entire shipment (they may be busy or shorthanded) a count shortage may go unnoticed. For example, a truck driver required to deliver 100 cases of a certain product may deliver only 90. If the shortage is noticed, the truck driver can readily acknowledge it and offer a plausible explanation. He or she may find the other 10 cases among other freight in the truck. Of course, the truck driver may be involved in a conspiracy with the victim's receiving dock personnel. When the 90 cases are delivered, they might sign for it as if 100 cases were delivered. If the victim's internal control system is not tightly structured, the 10 missing cases will always be a mystery, and warehouse theft will most likely be suspected.

An actual example of this occurred in warehouse, but was accidentally discovered during a shopping trip! The theft was discovered when an alert internal auditor, on his day off, happened to be shopping for bargains at a surplus sale in a commercial warehouse. While examining surplus furniture, he noticed several new desks that he liked. Upon examining them further, he noticed that the cartons bore standard government federal stock numbers (FSNs). He purchased one. When he returned to work the next day, he researched the FSN numbers and learned that the furniture items had only recently been introduced into the government's supply system and had never been sold as surplus. Further investigation revealed a conspiracy between the freight carrier and the receiving dock personnel. For example, if 100 items were to be delivered, the delivery service would drop off a lesser quantity, say 90. The conspirator on the receiving dock would certify that 100 had been received, the book inventory would be increased by 100, and the vendor would be paid for shipping 100—which the vendor did. The discovery of the scheme solved a long-standing mystery and explained the discrepancies noted for several years between physical inventory counts and the book inventory. It had been thought to be caused by thefts from warehouse stocks and/or defective shipments.

The basic prevention techniques for these types of fraud are essentially diligence and awareness. If goods are inspected upon delivery, randomly tested, and internal control policies followed up on, half the battle is won. Fraudsters are always looking for the weakest link, the disinterested clerk or someone "sleeping" on the job, the person who doesn't bother to check the quantities shipped, and so on. A conspiracy involving two or more people who purposely circumvent internal controls is much harder to catch, but mandating a basic level of diligence in verifying quantities is a big step in the right direction.

Defective Delivery of Labor

This fraud involves the substitution of less-qualified laborers than specified and invoiced. When an entity contracts for a specific category of skilled labor and is invoiced for that skill level, but receives a skill level lower than that agreed to, that is fraud. For example, if an entity wishes to have electrical work performed in a building and enters into a contract with an electrical contractor that specifies estimated hours of work by a master electrician at an hourly rate of, say $75 an hour, any work performed by an electrician of a lesser skill level could be fraud, if the less-qualified person was billed at the master electrician's rate. Consider the following case:

CASE 7.1   Contract Wage Costs Fraudulently Increased

A large computer software company contracted to provide system engineers to design a sophisticated new system. It was agreed that the contractor would be reimbursed on a time and material basis. The contract price was to be determined on the basis of the actual number of hours required to be billed at agreed-upon hourly rates for the various skill levels of computer engineers who would be assigned to do the work. That is, senior engineer hours would be reimbursed at, for example (not actual), $150 an hour, intermediate engineers at a rate of $100 an hour, and junior engineers at a rate of $75 an hour. The contract reserved the right to examine the contractor's records. The rates included overhead and profit.

A typical progress billing for hours expended resembled the following:

Period: January 20XX
Senior engineers:
I. P. Jones	160 hours @ $150 =	$24,000
Intermediate engineers:		
Al Smyth	200 hours @ $100 =	$20,000
Thomas Jepson	190 hours @ $100 =	19,000
Sheryl Upton	200 hours @ $100 =	20,000
Mary Shipp	200 hours @ $100 =	20,000
Barry Sullivan	75 hours @ $100 =	7,500
Junior engineers:		
John Maxtor	190 hours @ $75 =	$14,250
Bixby Fenster	35 hours @ $75 =	2,625
Total Costs January 20XX		$127,375

When internal auditors examined the computer company's records, they discovered that computer engineer skill classifications for Jones, Smyth, Shipp, and Sullivan were all correct as billed. However, Jepson and Upton were junior engineers and should have been billed at the $75 rate. This illustration is fictitious, but the fraud was real, and simplified here only to illustrate the finding. The actual fraud involved hundreds of thousands of dollars. The contractor, a nationally known company, was prosecuted and convicted.

Defective labor frauds are hard to prove unless you can get access to the supplier company's personnel and payroll records to document the experience level of employees. There are a few techniques that are low cost and can help prevent or detect fraud. One thing that can be done is to ask the suspected worker about their title or position in the company. Most times, management is perpetrating this type of fraud and the employee has no knowledge that they are being billed out at a higher rate. In this case, an honest answer from the worker about their position and title would be matched to the billing record. Also, proof of professional certifications, licenses held, or educational degrees can be requested before the job begins to see if the rates being charged are reasonable to the qualifications being asserted.

Defective Delivery of Building Construction

Over the years there have been many examples where building construction contractors have substituted inferior materials or taken other money-saving but harmful shortcuts in the supporting walls and supports of buildings and bridges under construction. When the buildings and bridges fail, the loss of life can be catastrophic and the architects and contractors involved are disgraced. Of course, these situations normally come to the public's attention only when the structures fail.

CASE 7.2   Building Construction Quality Degradation

A high-rise building was found to contain several serious defects, the most onerous of which was that the poured concrete walls of the structure were cold poured, whereas the construction contract required that the concrete walls be poured continuously. When concrete is poured continuously, all of the concrete—regardless of how much is poured—fuses together to form one solid, very strong block of material. This is most desirable for concrete walls to maximize their structural strength. The process is expensive, however, when much concrete must be poured, because considerable overtime and night differential wages must be paid over as many days as may be necessary to finish the wall.

The alternative is cold pouring the concrete. Basically, this means that concrete is poured into the forms until a convenient time to stop is reached. This may be at the end of a regular workday or at that point when it is necessary to erect additional forms. The concrete pouring process is resumed the next day. The problem is that the concrete that is poured the first day hardens before the next day's concrete can be poured. When pouring is resumed the next day, it is poured on top of the previous day's pour. Where the two pours meet, no fusing occurs, and a fault line is created. In effect, what happens is that two or more huge blocks of concrete are created, one sitting on top of the other. The fault line between the slabs weakens the structural strength of the wall, and under the right conditions—perhaps a mild earthquake—the wall can collapse. Conversely, perhaps it will never fail. However, fault line(s) in a building, especially over ten or more stories high, are very serious. In this particular case, the building contractor further weakened the walls by discarding scrap lumber into the wet concrete mix. The owner of the building chose never to pursue the defective delivery because it would require literally demolishing the structure and starting over.

Along similar lines, there was an interesting complication in another defective building construction case. The government, to ensure that the contractor complied with contract specifications—which required wet-pouring the concrete walls and no construction debris discarded into the concrete mixture—assigned a full-time engineer at the site to maintain surveillance over the construction process. This required the engineer to travel to the building site from his home, a considerable distance away, and return home each weekend. In effect, the on-site engineer was to be the quality control representative. His purpose was to ensure that the contractor complied with contract requirements. Foolproof? No. It seems the engineer had a mistress in a third city with whom he chose to spend his weeks away from home. His absence from the construction site allowed the building contractor to deviate from contract specifications as he chose.

Active internal controls depend on the integrity of the people who operate them, and they cannot always be relied on. The conclusion of this story is that the wayward engineer's deeds were discovered after the building was erected. He was allowed to resign without prosecution after he agreed to repay the travel and subsistence expenses he was given during the period he spent with his mistress. A large part of protecting the company against building construction fraud is to have a quality construction manager and team to monitor materials, processes, and progress on the project. If this critical component is not strong or breaks down as it did in this case, a large red flag is waving before the contractor inviting him to commit fraud.

A variation on defective delivery fraud requires a little advance planning on the perpetrators' part to include superfluous specifications in a contract or purchase order. As the product or service is being delivered, the superfluous features are eliminated. However, the vendor's invoice still includes the cost of the superfluous specifications, and the victim pays for them. The result is the delivery of a perfectly satisfactory product or service, which is not likely to raise objections or suspicions of inadequacy from users. In other words, although a defective delivery fraud may have occurred, the product or service delivered is in no way defective or otherwise unsatisfactory. The victim merely ends up paying for superfluous contract specifications never received. Because there is no defect, unless a proactive fraud investigator is clever and looks for this fraud, it is never discovered and there are no complaints. Again, a sharp construction manager would be expected to notice any changes in the contract or payment application submitted by the contractor and prepare change orders accordingly.

Detection Tips

Ordinarily, defective delivery fraud is not as difficult to detect as some of the other fraudulent activities. You need to determine that the product or service contracted for was delivered in all significant respects. Doing so requires a review of the contract or purchase order issued to determine exactly what was required and a comparison of one or more of the line items on it to the actual product or service delivered. (Often this process is more difficult to describe than it is to execute!) There is rarely a substitute for verification of actual delivery.

In some instances, especially where fraud may be involved, verification of delivery is not always so easy. In Chapter 6, under shell fraud, an example was presented where $450,000 was apparently spent remodeling an old medical clinic building. When trying to verify the improvements, it was found that the building had been torn down, eliminating the opportunity to see what was done. In such instances, each of which will have differing circumstances, you must be resourceful in verifying the satisfactory delivery of goods or services.

Internal controls will not receive major coverage in this text. However, as they specifically apply to the topics under discussion, they must be mentioned. Internal controls can be more effective than proactive examinations to control fraud, and you should identify opportunities where new internal controls would be beneficial in deterring or detecting fraud.

To control instances of one coat of paint being substituted for two coats, as was described previously, the tinted first coat idea is what is known as a passive internal control. The term passive is derived from the fact that once the control is initiated, it does not have to be maintained constantly. It merely exists and continues to serve its intended control purpose without any continuing cost or additional effort.

The tinted first coat of paint requirement, which costs little if anything to accomplish, does not prevent painters from applying only one coat. However, should they do so, the evidence of defective delivery of services remains ever-present and an effective indicator of fraud. It is telltale evidence of defective delivery just waiting to be discovered. Painters who claim that they did apply two coats of paint as required but simply forgot to tint the first coat, if not fraudulent, at the very least lose their proof that they applied two coats and should be reimbursed only for applying one coat. One mistake normally is insufficient basis for alleging fraud. However, if it is found that painters have "forgotten" to apply the tint more than once, a red flag is certainly raised.

In a sense, passive controls are analogous to land mines. Once the mines are buried on the perimeter of anything that must be protected, it is no longer necessary to actively guard that area quite as intensely. There is peril, or risk, for anyone choosing to enter the prohibited area. Another passive internal control that most accountants and auditors are familiar with is the so-called audit trail. The audit trail does not prevent fraud from happening, but it does allow internal and external auditors to backtrack a transaction trail to the beginning and hence, to the source that originated an entry of interest. Consequently, a perpetrator initiating a fraudulent accounting entry is always at risk of being identified through the audit trail that was left as a part of the permanent record. Passive internal controls do not prevent fraud but they do put perpetrators at risk, which often is sufficient to deter them—thus, expectation of being caught is raised and the element of opportunity is reduced.

Defective receipt fraud is similar to shell fraud in that victims pay for something they do not receive. Often verification procedures similar to those used to detect shell fraud can be used to detect defective deliveries. However, there is a significant difference between the two fraud types. In shell fraud, a fictitious purchase is involved and detection is normally relatively easy. Nothing is delivered, and often that fact can be determined readily. In defective receipt fraud, a legitimate purchase is involved, and a product or service is newly delivered, but victims do not get the full measure of the product or services ordered.

For example, if a contract called for carpeting an executive dining room, and shell fraud was involved, the dining room would not be newly carpeted, and a quick inspection would quickly establish this. In defective delivery fraud, the contract might require carpeting the dining room with $100-a-yard carpeting. The contractor's invoice would indicate that the dining room was carpeted with $l00-a-yard carpeting as specified, and the victim would pay the $100-a-yard carpeting price if a substitution was not detected. But let us assume that the dining room was, in fact, carpeted with $50-a-yard carpeting. Whereas in shell fraud, you would only need to look to see if new carpeting had been delivered, if defective delivery fraud had occurred, you would have to go beyond looking for a new carpeting installation to determine whether the contractor actually had delivered the $100-a-yard carpeting. To do this, you probably would have to obtain a sample of the carpeting and take it to an expert for appraisal, or engage an independent carpeting expert to visit the site. It also might be a good idea to recompute the number of square yards of carpeting required to carpet the dining room. Determining that the carpet buyer actually received the full quality and quantity of product required and invoiced often requires the services of experts. It cannot be stressed too often: You should not hesitate to hire such experts if verification of product or service delivery requires it.

DEFECTIVE SHIPMENT FRAUD

Defective shipment fraud involves the shipment or provision of the victim's products or services that (1) are superior in some manner and (2) do not include a corresponding increase in price to compensate the victim. The victim, of course, is not aware of the excess products or services being shipped or otherwise provided. Defective shipment fraud may involve everything from relatively petty fraud to large sums. Perhaps the greatest incidence of defective shipment fraud occurs in shipments from victims' warehouses. Whereas a shipping order may call for the shipment of 100 of some product, 110 are shipped. Whereas a grade B product should be shipped, a grade A product is substituted.

Retail merchants are frequent victims of defective shipment fraud, which may involve undercharging the customer (a conspirator) for products. Sales clerks are known to undercharge friends for items purchased. The widespread use of product UPC codes has limited the practice of this fraud somewhat. However, any enterprising thief need only have the UPC code from a cheaper product at the time an accomplice presents an item for payment. The clerk merely scans it to register a cheaper selling price. Accordingly, an accomplice presenting a $220 item at a cash register may be charged only $20 if the cashier scans a product code for the $20 item, resulting in a $200 loss in revenue for the merchant. Some merchants attempting to control this fraud routinely have a guard at exit doors to verify that the products sold were correctly charged— many high traffic electronics stores now employ a guard to check customer receipts and select items from the shopping cart to inspect at the exit.

In other instances, trusted employees substitute more costly materials or labor than those that were contracted for. This fraud type always involves conspiracy between an employee of the shipping entity and the recipient of the supplies or services that are being purchased. In some cases, victims are defrauded when dishonest employees fatten legitimate outgoing shipments from warehouses. This is possible because of weak internal controls or lax or dishonest employees responsible for administering controls, coupled with the victim entity's over-reliance on the effectiveness of internal controls without periodic verifications.

Active internal controls are the first line of defense against defective shipment fraud. However, active controls are much like chains: They are only as strong as their weakest links.

> *The gates are down, the lights are flashing, but the train isn't anywhere in sight.*[4]

Accordingly, although active internal controls are strongly advocated to prevent defective shipment fraud, they must not be totally relied on. Auditing, as a passive internal control procedure designed to periodically test the efficacy of active internal controls, is the most effective way of ensuring the prevention and/or deterrence of defective shipment fraud.

Accountants or auditors must periodically, on a surprise basis, observe or otherwise test internal control efficacy. They should determine that control personnel are rotated periodically and every so often, they should check the materials and/or supplies in the process of being delivered to determine that they are in agreement with warehouse shipping orders or sales orders. Where services are involved, auditors should periodically match invoices with personnel time cards to determine that the personnel services as billed were correctly charged.

DEFECTIVE PRICING FRAUD

Defective pricing fraud usually involves charging the victim a price higher than the price that was agreed on or falsely representing prices so as to deceive the victim. The fraud often is easily detected by proactive fraud investigations. An inside conspirator is almost always involved. In most instances, defective pricing fraud works very simply. A contractor and a contracting entity will enter into a contract to provide goods or services over a period of time, in accordance with prices set by the contract. The contractor periodically invoices the contracting entity at a higher price than that provided by the contract, and a conspirator—an employee of the contracting entity—approves the amount requested. If the conspirator is strategically placed, excessive billings are rarely questioned. This scheme can also be perpetrated with no conspirators, based on the lack of attentiveness and alertness of the company's employees, especially if there is a contract to provide hundreds or thousands of different parts or supplies, with each one having its own price.

For example, a utility had a contract with a local auto supply chain to provide auto parts for its fleet of vehicles. Each year, a price was set for each item to be purchased by the utility. However, because each invoice involved so many items for purchase, the purchasing department never bothered to check the prices they were being charged by the auto supply company. Forensic accountants later quantified thousands of dollars in over-charges; the auto supply company would simply charge the agreed upon rate for the first few months and then raise their rates. Nobody bothered to check the contract price for say, windshield wipers, which were invoiced at 10 to 15 percent higher than negotiated.

Usually the scheme is more complicated than simply agreeing to charge a set sum for some specific unit of services or goods. For example, the contract will not be so easily verifiable as to stipulate that the price for widgets ordered will be $150 each or the price of services delivered will be $100 per hour. Instead, more often these term contracts set the contract unit prices at something that reflects the market price, such as the contractor's most current published or catalog price for widgets, or an hour of service, all less 40 percent. Accordingly, contract negotiation usually dwells on the amount of the discount allowed rather than the unit prices charged.

In some instances, a vendor or contractor simply charges higher unit prices than those agreed to in the contract. Although most internal control systems require someone to review and approve an invoice before payment, many individuals charged with this responsibility tend to trust the companies submitting the invoices—

especially if they have been periodically rewarded with generous gratuities—and so they give the invoices a cursory review, if any at all. This is one of the hazards faced by employers who allow their employees to accept gratuities from vendors or contractors; or rather, companies who do not state in writing any kind of policy on this subject. To acknowledge the problem and possibly avoid it, at least partially, companies are well advised to adopt a zero gratuity policy.

CASE 7.3 The Disappearing Discount

This particular case began with a visit by Manufacturer X to the government's furniture procurement agency to solicit a large furniture contract. The manufacturer had been a producer of furniture for the government in the past and made essentially this offer:

"In return for a furniture contract for approximately $10 million, which would be our cost of production, we will waive our normal 10 percent profit of $1 million on the order. We make this offer to keep our factory busy, recover our overhead, and retain our employee workforce."

The government, which normally warehouses the furniture items offered for issue to government agencies, thought it was good business for both parties and gave the manufacturer the contract requested.

During the production period there were several changes to the design of the furniture being manufactured, which resulted in the need to hold a price renegotiation conference after the furniture had been completed, about two years later. Government personnel as well as those representing Manufacturer X sat around the negotiating table, while the manufacturer presented his price recapitulation. In addition to his total manufacturing costs of about $10 million, Manufacturer X added about 10 percent, or $1 million in profit. The government's contracting personnel reviewed the contract file, saw no reason to question the manufacturer's price summary, and adjourned the meeting for several days to prepare the final documents.

As luck would have it, an auditor had the opportunity to witness the renegotiation proceeding. He vaguely remembered the manufacturer's offer to waive his $1 million in profit but wasn't certain. The next day he returned to his office and reviewed the audit file on the contract. The auditor was a pack rat. He had saved a copy of everything that had taken place since inception of the contract, including a photocopy of the document signed by both parties agreeing to waive the $1 million profit. The manufacturer had substituted a similar document in his file that did not show that his profit had been waived. Interestingly, the copy of the document waiving his profit was also missing from the government's official file. The auditor's copy of the document prevailed, and the manufacturer's claim for $1 million in profit was denied. At the time this all happened, the question that seemed to defy solution was: Why didn't the government's file include the document that the auditor had in his file? An unrelated event that occurred six or seven years later suggested the answer. One of the officers of Manufacturer X was involved in the prosecution of another firm. During his questioning, it was revealed that Manufacturer X had been paying a government employee $500 a month to perform certain favors. Could he have removed the critical document from the government's files?

In pursuing defective pricing fraud, you should always become thoroughly familiar with the contractor purchase order terms and specifications. When examining invoices, you must make certain that all the terms were correctly applied to the invoice and that the contract or purchase order specifications agree with the contractor's or vendor's invoice.

For large contracts, internal auditors occasionally should extend the audit procedures to determine that the contract specifications are correct. That is, they should ensure that contract specifications were not altered after the contractor's proposal was accepted. This can be accomplished by examining the detailed price proposal submitted by the contractor when responding to the invitation for bids (IFB), if it is an advertised contract, or reviewing the records of negotiation if it is a negotiated contract.

SUMMARY

Remember, fraud is first and foremost committed by people, and no amount of internal controls will ever completely remove fraud from a business. The worst thing a company can do though, is to think "it could never happen to me." However, companies can significantly reduce the risk of fraud by being alert, diligent, and employing the appropriate internal controls for their business. Collusion in perpetrating fraud among employees or with others outside the company is always more difficult to detect. It often requires the services of an internal auditor or an outside investigator to uncover. Ultimately, the company has to set a strict tone and employ diligent controls to deter fraud and permit no tolerance for fraud if discovered. The company must maintain a healthy work environment in which the employees can maintain reasonable internal controls and diligence.

NOTES

1. http://www.brunswick.com/ethics/english/gifts.html.
2. http://w3.gsa.gov/web/p/hptp.nsf/0/f272892d7afc55c1852565c50054 b7f1?OpenDocument. See section 1.03(A.)3. of web site.
3. Vincent van Gogh, artist, 1853–1890; http://painting.about.com/library /biographies/blartistquotesvangogh.htm.
4. Anne Robinson, host of *The Weakest Link*, television game show.

8

CONTRACT RIGGING FRAUD

DEFINITION

"To rig" is defined by the *American Heritage Dictionary*,[1] in the context of contract rigging fraud, as "to manipulate dishonestly for personal gain." The term contract rigging is generally used to describe those clandestine and intentional acts that serve to give an unfair advantage to the contractor or rigger.

Although contracts are rigged, or manipulated, for criminal purposes in multiple ways, they always tend to involve a two-stage process. Stage 1 involves doing whatever is necessary to obtain the contract award. Stage 2 involves the actual mechanics of defrauding the victim. Contract rigging almost always involves conspiracy between an employee of the contracting entity and the contractor. Where contracts are rigged, the resultant fraud can be very significant in terms of dollar cost to the victim.

OBTAINING THE CONTRACT

The first objective of a perpetrator engaged in contract rigging fraud (CRF) is to obtain the award of the contract. This is absolutely necessary if the perpetrator is to gain the opportunity to fleece the victim.

Advertised Contract Awards

Most entities believe that the best way to protect themselves from fraud—and to ensure that they have obtained the lowest price for whatever it is they wish to acquire—is to advertise their intentions and to allow the marketplace to respond to their invitations to bid. They then select the lowest qualified bidder from those vendors or contractors who responded. The theory is that this practice allows the marketplace to determine the best contract price and ensures that the contractor will be selected impartially. Most entities, public and private, require the use of this advertising process in the naive belief that it protects their interests. They believe that interested contractors will sharpen their pencils and, in competing with each other, offer their lowest prices.

In a perfect world, this process probably would work very well. However, we do not live in a perfect world, and the process is flawed. Undoubtedly, many honest contractors do respond to IFBs on proposed major acquisitions. However, dishonest contractors are also likely to respond. And there are several ways that dishonest contractors are able to submit low price bids and win contract awards. Some involve plans to engage in defective delivery fraud to lower their cost expenditures by substituting cheaper materials and labor. Or, they may engage in contract rotation fraud, wherein a number of contractors will conspire to submit bids in response to an advertisement, allowing a chosen one of their number to submit the lowest bid, and to give the appearance of competition. On large contracts, however, contract rigging is a favorite practice of dishonest contractors.

Advertised Acquisition Process

When entities decide on a major acquisition, such as a construction project, for example, and are ready to select a contractor, they usually publish their intentions in a newspaper, on the Internet, or in other appropriate regional media to invite all prospective contractors who wish to compete to make their interest known to the advertising entity. Those contractors who express their interest are given IFBs, which include a complete set of blueprints, related specifications, and all information that may be necessary to allow each contractor to prepare cost estimates. Usually they are instructed to submit a sealed price proposal. Normally the advertising entity makes it known that the sealed bids submitted will be opened at a specified time and place. The lowest qualified bidder will be awarded the contract.

Getting the Contract Award

To gain the opportunity to rig the contract, any contractor intending to engage in contract rigging fraud must underbid all other bidders so as to be awarded the contract.

Submitting the lowest bid is rarely a problem for contractors planning CRF. There are two ways to ensure that they submit the lowest bid. The simplest way, if possible, is to have an accomplice—usually a key employee of the contracting entity—who will provide the amount of the lowest bid received from the other bidders. The contractor, of course, must delay submitting a bid until the very last moment. Then the contractor needs only to bid a small amount under the lowest bid to obtain the contract award. People rarely question a bid that is close to the other bids.

However, this procedure is rarely possible because in an effort to prevent CRF, most entities require that all bids received be sealed and opened in a public forum attended by all interested bidders, at a previously announced time and place. In such instances, there is no opportunity for an accomplice to observe the lowest bid and help a dishonest contractor undercut it.

When dishonest contractors can not gain the advantage of knowing the other bids submitted in advance, their submission of the lowest bid is made more difficult. However, they have an advantage because unlike the honest contracts, they do not have to submit a price proposal that will make a profit. In contract rigging fraud, the profit is realized in stage 2. Accordingly, preparation of a price proposal is dominated not by computations of what production costs are likely to be but by estimates of what other interested contractors are likely to bid, so that perpetrators do not bid so low that the bid appears totally unrealistic. Many bids submitted by CRF contractors would result in their financial ruin if they were required to meet the contract requirements as written. It is the rigging, which takes place in stage 2, that garners their profits.

In situations where inside conspirators are sufficiently influential, one scheme gives conspiring contractors an opportunity to know the prices other contractors have bid and gives them a second opportunity to adjust their prices after the sealed bid opening. In one large contracting action, the government sought to lease about 400,000 square feet of office space for a large agency. The specifications for their space needs were delivered to approximately six property owners who had expressed an interest in participating in the leasing action. About four property owners responded with sealed bids offering satisfactory office space, together with proposed rental rates. The four bids, expressed in terms of the square-foot rental rates per year, were: Bidder A: $18.95; Bidder B: $17.80; Bidder C: $17.50; and Bidder D: $17.17.

When the bids were opened and reviewed, someone decided that the original specifications given to the six interested landlords were unclear. To be "fair," it was decided that the ambiguity should be explained and all bidders should be given the opportunity to adjust their bids. A notice was sent out to all bidders with the clarified specifications, and all bidders were told that they would be permitted to resubmit their bids if they wished.

It became apparent that the specifications were not too ambiguous, because three of the bids returned were identical to the first bids submitted. Bidder C, however, who had originally bid $17.50, changed the bid to $17.16—one cent under the previous low bid. The original bid amounts submitted were supposed to have been held in confidence and not disclosed, except to personnel having a need to know. However, it seems obvious that the new low bidder had been informed by someone as to the amount of the previous low bid.

Not all low-price bids that appear to be suspiciously low are made with the intention of committing contract rigging fraud. For example, sometimes—due to a contracting entity's history of not being able to resist changing contract specifications—bidders may feel they can predict the contracting entity's future actions and will gamble that post-contract changes are likely to occur. Accordingly, they will offer a suspiciously low price, designed to win the contract award, a price they could never live with were they required to complete the contract without changes. However, no inside conspiracy may be involved and there may be no criminal manipulation. Contractors, based on past observations of the contracting entity's impulsive behavior, are gambling that the contracting entity will continue to tamper foolishly with contract specifications. Naturally, when that occurs, they will use the opportunity to revise their price. This does not constitute criminal behavior. If the entity does not change the contract, as the contractors hope, they would have to perform as required at the original price bid and they would probably lose money. These contractors, however, often have a fallback provision that allows them to declare bankruptcy (or do something less drastic) that enables them to escape from fulfilling the terms of the contract.

Many contracting entities cannot resist making changes to a contract after the initial award in order to incorporate afterthoughts to the specifications. Auditors are advised to review the contracting records of their employers or clients for evidence of this practice and firmly advise against it. Internal control systems should firmly require a no-contract-change policy or one that requires high-level approval by management.

The first objective of the CRF perpetrator is to secure the award of the contract. Nothing else is important. At the successful end of stage 1 of contract rigging fraud, no crime has yet been committed, except perhaps the act of conspiring to commit a crime. However, once stage 1 is complete, the perpetrator has gotten his proverbial foot in the door.

CONTRACT CHANGE ORDERS

Stage 2 of contract rigging fraud begins after the contract has been signed. Although fraudulent intent may be involved in stage 1, it is in stage 2 that the victim is actually fleeced. The contracting entity is defrauded in any number of ways, all of which involve contract specification change orders.

A contract is a legally binding agreement between two parties. In its simplicity, the contract agreement provides that contractors will deliver a specified product or perform a specified service, in return for which the contracting entity agrees to pay an agreed-upon sum.

The contracting entity often reserves the right to change the original contract specifications as necessary. When the contracting entity wishes to make a change to the contract, it prepares a document called a contract change order (CO). Sometimes when a product is undergoing specification changes, the change order is called an engineering change order (ECO). These orders usually are numbered sequentially and are referred to as CO1, CO2, and so forth. In the contract change order, the contracting entity specifies the exact nature of the changes it wishes the contractor to make, and the contractor must proceed to make them. However, it is always stated in writing that there will be a cost adjustment up or down as may be necessary to effect the changes, together with a renegotiation of prices to reflect any cost increases or decreases resulting from the contract changes. The contractor's cost of making the changes is usually fully reimbursable and left to be determined at some point after the contractor has completed the contract. Both parties to the contract are required under civil law to comply with contract change provisions.

Once a contract change order is issued, the contracting entity becomes vulnerable to whatever significant cost liability the dishonest contractor has planned. The entity initiating a contract innocently extends the opportunity for fraud merely by instituting contract changes. What the contracting entity does not know is that often, many of the changes are planned prior to the award of the contract by one or more of the entity's corrupt employees. Consider, for example, the pricing advantages available to a contractor who is aware of—and can depend on—major specification changes that will be made subsequent to the award of a contract. There are many ways contractors can adjust a price proposal to obtain the award of the contract and profit handsomely subsequent to the award. Among the things contractors can do are:

- Bid a low price on those contract items they are assured will be eliminated during the term of the contract.
- Defer work on contract items they know will be changed and falsely claim to have invested substantial sums in time and material, for which they are entitled to be reimbursed.
- Substitute cheaper materials than those specified.
- Unbalance the bid in such a way as to profit disproportionately as items are changed or eliminated.

Some entities strictly follow the practice of no changes after signing. However, most do not restrict changes as a matter of general practice. Where public entities are involved—such as federal, state, and local agencies—officials may have a fraudulent interest in seeing that the changes are made. Other organizations in which the managing officials are not a part of the vested ownership of the entities involved—such as colleges, universities, and hospitals— also may have similar interests and may, in fact, themselves be the inside conspirators who ensure contractors that certain changes will be made from which they all will be able to profit. To avoid this fraud peril, the general rule is to not enter into a contract unless you are absolutely sure that changes will not be necessary.

Entities that do change contract specifications expose themselves to a wide variety of fraud practices and should beware of becoming victims. Of course, all contract specification changes do not incur fraudulent intent, but all are risky. Obviously, there are many honest contractors who will submit the fair cost of any changes made. However, even honest contractors may find it hard to resist the opportunity to recover costs and profits that may have been lost in competitive bidding and cost-shaving. Once again we confront opportunity and expectation, which may the swing the pendulum for those not inherently honest.

When a contracting entity decides to alter the specifications of an existing contract, two events occur: The contracting entity must formally change the contract's requirements, and it must provide for an appropriate adjustment in the contract price. The amount of the adjustment cannot be computed until after the required change is completed. This is as it should be. However, at this point the contracting entity is at the mercy of the contractor. The contracting entity has lost any advantage originally gained when the contract was competitively advertised, when bidding contractors were constrained in price proposals by competition. Once a contract has been awarded and changes are made, there are no such natural price restraints. The contract change order is, in effect, a sole source contract. When contracting entities require changes, they no longer have the option of choosing another contractor and the contractor can, at the very least, be expected to be generous in his or her own behalf in recovering all costs and profits. For dishonest contractors, being given a change in contract requirements is like being given the combination to the bank vault.

Change Orders to Correct Omissions

It is not uncommon for a contracting entity to fail to include all features of a construction project in the specification package mailed out to contractors. When this occurs, and when the omission is not detected before the specifications package is mailed out to prospective bidders, contractors are likely to prepare their bids for a complete, all-inclusive structure often by relying heavily on statistical costs to prepare their cost estimates (e.g., $100 per square foot). After all bids are received, the lowest qualified bidder is awarded the contract and authorized to proceed with construction.

As actual contract work gets under way and specification omissions are discovered and brought to the customer's attention, the customer has no choice but to issue a contract change order(s) to include the missing specifications in the contract. Were the change order not written, contractors would be perfectly within their rights to construct the building as originally specified, even though the plans were deficient. Contract change orders covering the missing specifications require contractors to comply. However, because the change orders specify work that was not in the original specification package on which the contractors bid, they are entitled to add the extra costs to the contract price. Sometimes the omissions are unintentional, and in such instances no fraud may be involved.

However, if contractors were aware of the omission at the time they prepared the price proposal, this knowledge would allow them to reduce their estimated price for the construction and give them a pricing edge in the competitive bid—an edge that contractors who did not detect the omission would not have. More to the point, if the omission was not readily apparent, if perhaps it was intentionally omitted, and one bidding contractor was informed as to the nature of the missing specification, he or she would have a clear advantage over other bidders. That contractor would be able to underbid the others, knowing that there would be a later opportunity to add back any costs that were eliminated in the competition to be low bidder.

Experienced forensic accountants view all contract change orders with a sense of wariness. They will be immediately concerned about whether the omission was accidental or planned. If it appears to have been planned, fraud bells and whistles will begin to sound and the entire contract will be suspect and will require a critical examination.

Assuming there were no further irregularities in the contract, at the very least, the contracting entity would have lost any advantage received through the competitive bidding process and may end up paying a costly premium for the omission. However, where significant omissions have occurred and the omissions were planned for fraudulent purposes, it would be surprising if the contracting entity did not experience a need for more changes as the contractor's work continues.

Specification Change Orders

Some entities, when constructing a new building, follow a strictly hands-off or turn-key policy. These terms mean that, once the contract has been awarded, the architect and/or contractor are responsible for delivering a fully functional building for the agreed-upon price. The entities take the self-protective attitude that the architect and/or contractor should have exercised due care before the contract award. They contend that by submitting the completed blueprints and/or contract bids, the architect and/or contractor became responsible for performance in accordance with them. The entities want nothing to do with construction problems and avoid any involvement with the construction until the architect or contractor gives them the keys to open the completed building. If there is a need to change a specification that was not foreseen by the architect, the entity's attitude is: "It is the architect's responsibility, he or she should bear the cost." Entities take these attitudes to protect themselves from cost increases, problems of any sort encountered during construction, as well as contract rigging fraud. Should any problems result in contract delivery delays or cost claims, they are prepared to enforce the terms of the contract that call for a completed building at an agreed price at a specified time. The downside of this policy is that architects and contractors who accept this degree of risk are apt to charge more for taking it, increasing the cost of the construction.

However, few entities can actually restrict themselves to a hands-off approach. They tend to be drawn into the construction details, changing building features sometimes capriciously and exposing themselves to a multitude of abuses. Sometimes their changes are the result of innocent second thoughts or omissions, but sometimes the changes are premeditated by inside conspirators to produce the opportunity to fleece the contracting entity. In the following case, consider what happened during the construction. Were the changes honest and sincere or were they fraudulently inspired? This is a true story.

CASE 8.1   The Construction in Progress Specification Change

A six-story building was in the process of being constructed. The contract had been advertised. After several months had elapsed, the tenant that was to occupy the building stated it wanted a minor change in the building's design. After reviewing the directional siting on the property, it decided it wanted to take advantage of morning sunlight through a laboratory's windows, and insisted the building be rotated clockwise on the site about 90 degrees. Because none of the building's foundation or superstructure had yet been built, the request was granted, and a contract change order was issued.

Much later, when the time came for the contractor to submit the costs incurred as a result of the change in plans, they were substantial. The construction contractor claimed he had already installed all underground utilities (water, sewer, electrical), which had to be redone when the building site plan was rotated away from its original site. In addition to claiming the cost of installing new underground utilities, he claimed all of the costs he incurred in installing the underground utilities as originally specified. His claim was perfectly legitimate and it had to be paid. However, the circumstances certainly presented an opportunity for padding his expenses.

A fraud examination was never performed in response to the indicia suggested by the circumstances just described. However, had one been done, the fraud examiner would surely have attempted to resolve the following questions:

- Did the contractor actually install the underground utilities that he claimed became redundant when the new contract change order was issued? If he had reason to suspect that the building site would be changed at the start of the contract, he could have delayed installing the underground utilities to the original site and later could have claimed he had installed them, charging for the utilities to the original site as if they actually were installed. How could he be aware of the coming change?

There are several possibilities, all of which would have required a bit of advance planning. For example, the architect may have known that the new building's tenant was vulnerable to the suggestion that the building's laboratories face toward the southeast to catch the morning sun. To take advantage of this vulnerability, he need only design the building with its laboratories facing northeast. It would be very easy subsequently to plant that idea in the tenant's mind. This scheme, of course, would require collusion between the architect and the contractor.

A dishonest contractor would not have installed any underground utilities to the original location site if he was aware of the impending contract change order, and particularly if he was conspiring with the architect. He would simply delay installing the utilities, or even perhaps install the utilities in the location needed to best serve the expected new building site. His false claim would be totally unfounded, but at the time he would be most likely to file it, it would be very difficult to prove it was false.

- Was the prospective tenant a conspirator to the fraud suggested here? If the tenant was influential in the building's original site, as can be expected, his or her subsequent change of heart is at the very least suspicious and certainly would have been enabling.
- Is there any evidence that the contractor or architect were aware of the tenant's site wishes before the bid proposals were submitted? If so, this information could have given the contractor an unfair advantage in preparing his price proposal.

You should consider the possibility that architects may be coconspirators in fraud, designing or omitting construction features that will subsequently require contract changes, providing the opportunity for costly, perhaps fraudulent claims. However, you must also determine the general design specifications that architects were given by their clients.

When something goes wrong in the construction of a building, some of the questions a fraud investigator would be likely to ask include:

1. Who determined the tenant occupancy plan for the new building?
2. To what degree was the architect independent in his or her initial building design, versus responding to the contracting entity's design orders?
3. Was the contracting entity responsible for requiring unnecessary changes after construction had begun, or were the changes the result of evolving circumstances?
4. Were the changes premeditated to provide the contractor an opportunity to submit supplementary cost claims?

5. How many of the supplementary cost claims were bona fide costs incurred as the result of contract changes, and how many were falsely claimed by the contractor?

6. Are all of the above true?

There is nothing intrinsically wrong with changing a contract's specifications. However, when contract rigging is involved, the changes to contract specifications are opportunities fraud perpetrators look for. Many changes are premeditated and often initiated—directly or indirectly—by a key employee of the contracting entity. For the perpetrators, timing of changes is crucial; they must be initiated at a point when contract work-in-progress is substantial so that the contracting entity has no practical alternatives to costly charges.

Post-Award Change Orders

Contract rigging with fraudulent intent occurs in the acquisition of personal property as well as real property. Most of the mechanics in personal property fraud are very similar to that involving real property. The fraud usually occurs in the acquisition of personal property manufactured to the entity's specifications, as opposed to off-the-shelf items. The entity's interest in purchasing custom-made personal property is made known to the relevant manufacturing community. Those manufacturers interested in competing are provided with manufacturing specifications. Manufacturers submit price proposals. The lowest qualified bidder is awarded the contract to manufacture the items. Any changes after the contract is awarded are accomplished through change orders.

Product Degradation

Surely everyone has seen old movies where someone is given a gold coin in payment for something. The recipient frequently bites the coin to verify if it was gold. Obviously, he is concerned that someone will substitute a cheaper metal for the more valuable gold. Base metals such as lead have been substituted for precious metals such as gold. Anyone who has any doubt as to the profit to be made in substituting lead for gold need only to look at the commodities market on any given day. For example, gold was worth about 10,000 times the price of lead, yet a government contractor substituted lead for gold in a defense contract, claiming that there was no cost effect in recommending the engineering change to the U.S. Navy. The details are relayed in the following case.

Case 8.2   Easily Lead?

This story begins with a contractor—Contractor X—who obtained a government contract to build an antiaircraft missile for the navy. The initial contract was sole source (given without competition) to a very capable aerospace contractor to design and build a long-range missile having certain prescribed defense capabilities not then existing in the navy's arsenal. Of course, no specifications existed that could be advertised. Customary in such instances, the contract was fully cost reimbursable.

Contractor X labored for several years in designing and building prototype missiles. Using design recommendations provided by a major university, the contractor ultimately constructed a missile that ended up being very effective with a high target acquisition rate. As is usual with cost-reimbursable contracts of this type, no expense was spared to build the very best missile to heighten its dependability in acquiring and destroying enemy targets many miles away from the fleet. As cost was secondary to quality, the highest-grade components were used, including nickel and gold plating on electrical circuit board pathways.

After several years and many millions of dollars spent on design, engineering, and prototype construction, the missile specifications had evolved sufficiently and were enduring enough to justify a large production contract. The navy, interested in obtaining the best possible production price, decided to advertise the contract, and solicited price proposals from several major manufacturers, one of which was Contractor X.

Prior to this time, Contractor X had no real incentive to reduce manufacturing costs. Production had not been cost effective, and Contractor X quickly realized that its prior extravagant production experience would be a liability rather than an advantage. If it were to win the advertised contract award, Contractor X would have to offer a price that would underbid a very competitive marketplace, and that would be difficult. Nevertheless, it did. It bid what it believed to be a low competitive price—one that was considerably under its previous costs per missile produced under the cost-reimbursable contracts. Its proposed price was the lowest bid, and it was awarded a production contract of about $100 million.

However, it did not take Contractor X long to realize that it would lose money if it was required to build the missile at the price bid. And, shortly after the contract was awarded, a group of Contractor X's engineers found themselves in meetings to discuss ways and means of sufficiently reducing the cost of manufacturing the missile to enable the company to make a profit. The engineers suggested various ideas for changes that would reduce costs. Many of the suggested changes eliminated parts, modified physical design of the parts, substituted cheaper materials, relaxed acceptance tolerances, and reduced prescribed testing. Generally, the changes served to make the missiles much less expensive to produce.

The problem with the cost reduction changes that were suggested (aside from the fact that the changes would result in a degraded product) was that the contract bid price for building the missiles was based on the higher missile specifications existing at the time the contract was advertised. Any cost reductions that would result from making them should have been passed on to the U.S. Navy and should not have benefited Contractor X—unless, of course, the firm's owner was deceitful, and that is exactly what it appears he was.

Government auditors discovered details that revealed the contractor's intention to cut production costs and hence profit from its low bid. Their report revealed the contractor was trusted to designate which engineering changes were major in nature (Class I) and would require a comprehensive review by navy engineers, and which were minor (Class II) and not subject to extraordinary review. This of course was a rather naive internal control plan, and somewhat akin to giving the keys to the chicken house to the fox. Contractor X simply designated many of the engineering specification changes which resulted in the missile's degradation as Class II changes, thereby avoiding scrutiny of its claims that no cost reductions were involved. The changes were approved by a mid-level naval officer in residence at Contractor X's manufacturing plant, without any questions as to the serious nature of the changes or the cost effect. The office apparently had no problems with Contractor X's claim that the substitution of a tin/lead alloy in lieu of a nickel/gold alloy plating would result in no cost savings. The auditors computed a $50,000 savings in materials to Contractor X from this single change. In another of the several hundred Class II changes made by the contractor, the officer apparently had no problem approving Contractor X's claim that no cost savings would result from the change from hand-soldering electrical circuit board connections to simply passing the assembled circuit boards over molten lead (flow soldering). The auditors discovered that the change was expected to result in a 94 percent reduction in soldering labor.

In an interesting postscript to the missile illustration, the navy eventually became so alarmed at the precipitous loss of their missile's reliability in test firings that it gave an engineering study contract to Contractor X to determine the reasons for the performance degradation. After an appropriate period of time to study the defective missiles, Contractor X essentially recommended reversals of the cost-cutting changes it had made during the production of the missile inventory.

This is a classic case of contract rigging. Contractor X was in a unique position that few contractors enjoy. Not only did the company manufacture the missiles, it also served as the designer of the missiles. Accordingly, it was understandable that when Contractor X recommended what it described as minor engineering changes to the navy—in its authoritative role as the missile's designer—the recommendations were readily accepted. What cannot be as easily explained is why the resident navy officer approved the recommended design changes as submitted, even though they were obviously not minor, as classified, and even though Contractor X submitted them with the notation "no cost effect," when certainly most if not all of the changes obviously involved labor and material cost savings. Do you smell a conspiracy here?

UNBALANCED BIDDING

Unbalanced bidding fraud is a type of contract rigging in which a contractor planning to perpetrate fraud bids a price estimated to be lower than any of the other bidders, and on which they probably would lose money if they were required to complete the contract advertised at the price bid. However, such contractors are counting on the occurrence of certain events that will restore profits, and more. Unbalanced bidding fraud is similar to the other contract rigging frauds previously discussed except for one important aspect. It is considerably more subtle and is easy to overlook.

In the other types of contract rigging frauds, perpetrating contractors depend on contract change orders that add new requirements and open the door for price negotiations in which they expect to charge outrageous prices and recover costs and profit. In unbalanced bidding fraud, contractors anticipate that the contracting entity will cancel a requirement and, as a result, leave them with a handsome profit.

In unbalanced bidding, fraud contractors customarily overprice one or more line items while they sufficiently underprice other line items so that their aggregate bid is likely to be the low bid. Such bidders are anticipating that the items they lowball on will be canceled from the contract, leaving only the overpriced items to manufacture, which will provide a handsome profit.

Case 8.3 is a very oversimplified illustration of unbalanced bidding fraud.

CASE 8.3   A Simple Case of Unbalanced Bidding

Assume that the Yore Corporation wishes to have a freight transfer terminal (Building A), a warehouse (Building B), and a service workshop (Building C) constructed. All three buildings must be completed by December 31 of the current year. A penalty of $5000 per day will accrue for each day subsequent to December 31 that final delivery is delayed. The three contractors interested in participating (Contractor Dewey, Contractor Cheatham, and Contractor Howe) are provided with the building specifications and instructed to submit their price proposals by line item. Building A is line item 1, Building B is line item 2, and Building C is line item 3. The Yore Corporation reserves the right to change contract specifications or delete items at any time, and to renegotiate prices as may be necessary as a result of any changes it may make.

The contractor price proposals received were:

Contractor Dewey:

Line Item 1	$100,000
Line Item 2	$195,000
Line Item 3	$225,000
TOTAL BID	$520,000

Contractor Cheatham:

Line Item 1	$105,000
Line Item 2	$203,000
Line Item 3	$229,000
TOTAL BID	$537,000

Contractor Howe:

Line Item 1	$132,000
Line Item 2	$135,000
Line Item 3	$243,000
TOTAL BID	$510,000

Before reading further, please take a few minutes to contemplate these bids. Keep in mind the following:

- Fraud may not be present in this transaction at all. It may be a trick to cause readers to speculate on fraud they expect to be there when in fact none is present.

- Given only the above information, assuming that each contractor is equally qualified, who should get the contract? Why?

- If anyone other than the low bidder was chosen, reasoning must be justified.

At this point in the contract, there is nothing apparently wrong with the bids received. Contractor Howe has offered the lowest price and must be accepted. This contractor is qualified and offers a price $10,000 lower than the next lowest bidder. Mary Lande is an official in the Storage Division. Ms. Lande is aware that the corporation is growing very rapidly and seriously lacks adequate storage space. She had known

Charlie Howe, the Contractor Howe owner, since they were in high school together, over 22 years ago. At their last high school reunion she attracted Charlie's interest when she casually mentioned that Yore Corporation was going to build several new buildings estimated to cost over $500,000. As a building contractor, Charlie was interested in getting the job, and Mary mentioned it would be advertised.

The next day Charlie called Mary and they had lunch together. Charlie reminded Mary that she had said the warehouse would probably be too small before it was completed, and asked why a larger building was not being built. Mary replied that she planned to recommend just that before the specifications were mailed out for bids. She said that since the building had been planned last year, the Yore Corporation had experienced a surge in manufacturing that predictably would continue. Charlie replied that building a warehouse twice as large would not cost that much more. Mary agreed and said that she did not think it would be difficult to sell the larger building to corporation management. She said she would begin immediately, to which Charlie replied, "Wait, I've got an idea. Why not wait a few months until after the contract is awarded, and then do it?" He explained his plan to submit a low bid, pricing the warehouse low to get the contract. Then when she was successful in selling the corporation on a larger warehouse, he predicted he could net well over $50,000 when the smaller warehouse was canceled from the contract and the larger warehouse was added. He offered to split the $50,000 with Mary. Mary agreed, and everything worked according to plan. Charlie turned out to be the low bidder.

After the contract was awarded to Howe, the Yore Corporation notified him to begin construction of Building A immediately. Several weeks later, Mary reported to the Yore Corporation management board that the construction of Building A was proceeding well. She also voiced her concerns that given their excellent sales forecasts, the new warehouse building would very likely be obsolete before it was finished. One of the management officers suggested, "The new warehouse construction hasn't yet been started yet, so we have an excellent opportunity to build a larger building."

Everyone agreed and item 2 on Contractor Howe's contract was ordered canceled and the contract price reduced by the amount he had bid—$135,000. Mary bought a new Buick with the $25,000 Charlie gave her.

The Yore Corporation received its annual audit the following January. By chance, the auditors examined the construction contract for the three buildings, saw it had been advertised; the lowest bidder selected, and took no audit exceptions.

DETECTION RECOMMENDATIONS

Contract rigging fraud, if crafted carefully, is very difficult to detect or to take action against on a timely basis. The important thing, as with all fraud, is to know that it exists and to be watchful for signs of it. Although it is often possible to discern what appear to be (1) suspicious bidding practices or (2) unbalanced bidding in stage 1, little can be done to change anything. If a bidder chooses to offer an unusually low bid, one that will lose money, that is the bidder's prerogative. It is not the advertising entity's responsibility to ensure that the bidder makes a profit. However, when suspicious stage 1 bidding practices or apparent profit-loss bids are observed, you should view them as possible precursors to fraud. What to do about them is the question. The answer is to watch what may come next very carefully.

In almost all instances where contract rigging fraud is suspected, contract changes are the keys to the perpetrator's success. Stop the contract changes and you will likely go a long way toward stopping contract rigging fraud. The contract must be changed in some way for the perpetrator to profit. Of course, it is the anticipation of the changes that causes the perpetrator to bid low in the first place as they never expect to have to do the job at the price bid. Always remember that as long as the suspect contract remains unchanged, it is usually very difficult for CRF perpetrators to profit. Accordingly, financial managers, accountants, auditors, or whoever is looking for contract rigging fraud should become a bit paranoid with regard to all contract changes, both those proposed before the fact and those executed after the fact.

If suspicious bidding practices or unbalanced bidding are suspected, extra attention should be given to any contract changes proposed by the contracting entity. Such changes should be carefully scrutinized to determine who proposed the changes, the cost effect of the changes, and any other consequences on the overall contract. Every attempt should be made to determine the cost of the change, including a requirement that the contractor prepare an estimate of what the costs of making the change are likely to be. Where the changes will have a harmful effect on overall contract cost, entity management should be made aware of the consequences.

If the changes are required because of a design error, you need to find out who was responsible for the error. Is it the architect? If so, he or she may be responsible for any extraordinary costs incurred. Also, you should make every attempt to pinpoint the source of any changes originating within the entity. In other words, does the contractor have an inside conspirator who may be instrumental in generating the changes? Is there any reason to believe that a contract change was known or could have been anticipated at the time the contract was advertised, which could have been communicated to the bidding contractor to allow him or her to lower the bid and win the contract? In other words, is there any evidence to indicate when the idea for the change was first conceived? How does that date compare with the bid solicitation dates?

Skeptics with a reason to suspect contract occurrences but who cannot prove anything might consider reviewing past contracts or

purchase orders that involved the contractors and/or insiders suspected of involvement. If they are guilty of wrongdoing, chances
are a pattern will be evident in past events. Any patterns developed
may make or at least strengthen your convictions.

ROTATION FRAUD

Rotation fraud is a close cousin to contract rigging fraud. In rotation fraud, two or more contractors who dominate an industry in a
region conspire to alternate the business between them, thereby de-
feating the advantages of advertised contracts. They obviously feel
that it is preferable to share the business equally rather than to engage in cutthroat competition where everyone loses profits.

In there are three contractors involved, for example, they will
conspire as to whose turn it is to win an advertised contract, Contractor A, Contractor B, or Contractor C. If it is Contractor B's turn,
then Contractor B will bid a comfortable price with an ample profit,
making the bidding price known to Contractors A and C. Contractors A and C will then slightly overbid, thus giving the appearance
of competition. The contracting entity is pleased and believes it has
received the best price available in the marketplace, which is evident in the closeness of the prices offered. Normally, when rotation
fraud occurs, there is no conspirator involved within the contracting
entity's ranks.

In a variation of rotation fraud, only one contractor participates
in a bidding action, conspiring with the contracting entity's procurement agent to provide false documentation giving the appearance that three or more contractors submitted bids. Anyone
reviewing the procurement files after the fact will find that the procurement action was advertised, that three contractors responded
with bids, and the lowest bidder was chosen. End of story!

It is very difficult to detect or to stop rotation fraud. Rarely is an
insider conspiracy involved, except possibly in the situation just described. All the documentation is genuine, as are the contractors

who have submitted bids. One recommendation that is worth pursuing is to perform background checks on bidders to assess whether any relationships exist that may represent a conflict. Another recommendation is to determine all contractors who should have been interested in bidding on this contract. If, for example, a painting contract is involved, auditors should check who the painters in the general area are and from whom the entity should have received bids, but did not. If the list contains more names than those from whom bids were received, auditors might contact them and ask why they did not bid on the solicitation. Auditors should use their best and most congenial interviewing technique, give them an opportunity to talk, and listen very carefully to what they have to say. They may never have known about the solicitation, in which case auditors should find out why. There may be political reasons why they did not bid. Perhaps they were intimidated out of the competition. Auditors should get as many details as possible, and follow any leads provided.

NOTE

1. *American Heritage Dictionary of the English Language, Fourth Edition,* 2000, Boston: Houghton Mifflin, January 15, 2000.

9

ETHICAL BEHAVIOR

What is ethical behavior? The *Encyclopedia Britannica* defines ethics as the "branch of philosophy concerned with the nature of ultimate value and the standards by which human actions can be judged right or wrong."[1] Ethics is not simply a theoretical philosophy; children and adults in every walk of life make ethical decisions every day. When someone enters the workforce, they bring with them a personal ethical code that must be integrated into the workplace.

Business ethics examines moral controversies relating to the social responsibilities of business practices in any economic system.[2] Ethical business behavior is determined by the interaction of professional standards, the law, government regulations, industry practices, cultural and social mores, and perhaps most importantly, one's own internal moral code. In this chapter, we discuss ethical behavior on the part of accounting professionals investigating frauds, and the importance of establishing a business Code of Conduct.

ACCOUNTING ETHICAL STANDARDS

Professional accounting/business standards, which address ethical behavior, abound. The AICPA, the Securities and Exchange Commission, State Boards of Accountancy, Department of Labor, and the Government Accounting Office, among others, have standards dictating ethical behavior as related to accounting and business practices. In addition, many professional publications have monthly features on business ethics. Some examples of professional ethics resources follow:

- The AICPA *Code of Professional Conduct* ("The AICPA Code") was established to provide rules to all members, including those in public practice, as well as industry, government, and education, to be applied in the performance of their professional responsibilities.[3] Some of the major topics covered by the Code are:
  - Independence
  - Due Professional Care
  - Confidentiality
  - Contingent Fees
  - Advertising
  - Commissions and Referral Fees

Specific questions on professional ethics and legal responsibilities of accountants are included on the CPA exam.

- The AICPA Professional Ethics Executive Committee ("The Committee") is charged with the responsibility of interpreting and enforcing The AICPA Code. The Committee (1) investigates potential disciplinary matters involving members; (2) arranges for the presentation of a case before the joint trial board where the committee finds prima facie evidence of infraction of the bylaws or The AICPA Code; and (3) interprets The AICPA Code.[4]
- All State Boards of Accountancy have established ethical codes or standards of conduct. Most of these codes can be accessed through the Internet and should be reviewed along with The AICPA Code.
- Sarbanes-Oxley: Section 406 requires that the Securities and Exchange Commission (SEC) issue rules to require public

companies to disclose whether or not they have adopted a code of ethics for senior financial officers including its principal financial officer, comptroller, principal accounting officer, or persons performing similar functions. If a company does not have a code of ethics that meets the requirements of the new rules, the company must disclose in its annual report the reasons why it has not adopted a code of ethics. The term code of ethics is defined as such standards as are reasonably necessary to promote:

- Honest and ethical conduct, including handling of actual or apparent conflicts of interest between personal and professional relationships;
- Full, fair, accurate, timely, and understandable disclosure in the periodic reports required to be filed; and
- Compliance with applicable governmental rules and regulations.[5]
- The Securities and Exchange Commission. On January 15, 2003, the SEC adopted rules implementing Section 406 of the Sarbanes-Oxley Act of 2002. Some legal experts have concluded that the SEC believes that the "codes of ethics should vary from company to company and that decisions regarding the exact contents of a company's code of ethics, compliance procedures and disciplinary measures are best left to each individual company."[6] Adoption of codes of ethics that are more comprehensive and more detailed than the minimum necessary to fulfill the new regulatory requirements is clearly a good idea.

Certainly accounting and business ethics have the attention of lawmakers, regulatory authorities, and professional associations. Your responsibility as an accounting professional is to know and adhere to the appropriate standards. Some requirements are based on your professional designation. CPAs must abide by AICPA and state Codes. Those individuals who are in senior management positions must be aware of and adhere to all relevant Sarbanes and SEC requirements. These standards and interpretations of the standards can and do change. The volume of relevant laws, pronouncements, and regulations may seem daunting but it is your responsibility to understand and follow the standards that are applicable to you.

CONSEQUENCES OF UNETHICAL BEHAVIOR

The consequences of not following these laws, regulations, and standards are severe. For example, CPAs can lose their licenses. Formal processes to file complaints against professionals who do not comply with standards of ethical behavior exist. Civil and criminal actions can be initiated by the Department of Justice, the SEC, and local prosecutors, among other organizations.

The AICPA has established a Joint Ethics Enforcement Program (JEEP) with the state CPA societies for ethical enforcement. The program's objectives are to provide (1) a single investigation and action; and (2) uniformity in the codes of conduct of the AICPA and state societies; and (3) uniformity in the enforcement and implementation of the codes of conducts. *The JEEP Manual of Procedures* can be downloaded from the AICPA web site.[7]

We have covered the governing bodies but here is the true question: If you comply with all the regulatory bodies, are you behaving ethically? While all of these agencies will provide guidance, they cannot predict every situation with its complexities and uniqueness, so any practitioner's ethical behavior will ultimately include his or her personal morality and social behavior.

CODES OF CONDUCT

A code of conduct, sometimes referred to as a standard of conduct, is written to establish a company's expectations of business ethics and regulatory compliance and to assist employees dealing with situations where the "right" answer is not always clear. As previously discussed, a formal code of conduct is now a requirement of public companies mandated by the Sarbanes-Oxley Act (Sarbanes). The requirements mandated by Sarbanes are discussed more fully in Chapter 3.

After a business has determined that it has complied with the relevant legal and regulatory requirements, a business should consider developing a specific, detailed, written code of conduct over and above the minimum legal requirements. A code of conduct should include a clear statement of what behavior is acceptable and what behavior is not acceptable. Finally, it should state the consequences if the standards are breached. It goes without saying that management must also demonstrate that if the standards are not followed, all employees are subject to the same consequences. In other words, be prepared to enforce the standards, no matter who violates them.

Acknowledge the Code

To be effective, the code of conduct must be required reading for all employees at least once every year and employees must be required to sign that they have read and understood the standards provided. From that point forward, employees who have been compelled to read the standards are bound to comply with them, regardless of what their personal views on ethical behavior may be. Even though every employee, depending on his or her own private criteria for what is right or good and driven by the wide range of differences in moral character, will have different limits (if any) on personal behavior, the employer's published code of conduct is binding on employees during the hours of their employment. An effective code of conduct should include the consequences for a breach in policy and the necessary disciplinary action that will be taken. These consequences could include termination of employment and criminal prosecution, if warranted. Management should review the standards periodically to determine if they should be revised.

Why Are Codes of Conduct Important?

Nothing can ensure that all employees will behave ethically. However, companies that create an atmosphere of honesty, convey the importance of ethical behavior, behave ethically, and clearly advertise the consequences of unethical behavior have a much better chance of fostering honest employees. When management issues a code of conduct, it sets the tone that they take ethical behavior seriously.

The failure of employers to declare and publish definitive standards of conduct for their employees to follow is equivalent to allowing employees to use their own judgment, which of course, allows some employees to stretch the limits to justify their errant behavior.

What is Included in a Company's Code of Conduct?

There is no standard code of conduct. Each company must evaluate its business and develop its own realistic standards; recognizing that legal, regulatory, and professional requirements must always be met. A typical code of conduct might include a statement from the CEO about the ethical conduct of the company, guidelines for handling of conflicts of interest (i.e., accepting gifts from customers or vendors, related party transactions, borrowing from the corporation, etc.), prohibitions and/or restrictions on the use of confidential information, and corporate policies (i.e., expense policies, vacation policies, insider trading, etc.). Other employee behavioral standards—including policies regarding lateness, vacations, outside employment, or fraternization between employees, for example—could be expressed in the company's standards of conduct. The entity's policy on employee use of computers and copying equipment for personal reasons also should be clearly stated.

Gifts, Gratuities, Bribes—Is There a Slippery Slope?

Of particular importance in any written codes of conduct is a discussion regarding the acceptance of things of value by employees from entities doing business with the employer. These items of value are commonly considered gifts and sometimes are called gratuities. They range from items of little or no monetary value, such as a calendar or a free lunch, to things of considerable value, such as large cash amounts, automobiles, and expensive vacations.

Although many employees who receive gratuities might argue that the gratuities received do not influence them to favor the entity giving the gratuity, most employers have good reason to think otherwise. It is interesting to note that although the conveniently popular understanding of a gratuity is that it is something of value given without the expectation of something in return, the formal definition of a gratuity is: "a favor or gift, usually in the form of money, given in return for service"[8] Employers who may be considering prohibiting their employees from accepting gratuities should ask themselves: "Gratuities given in return for what service?" And readers should ask themselves: "When was the last time someone other than a friend or relative who was not indebted to me bought me an expensive lunch without wanting something in return?"

Should entities considering the adoption or modification of their codes of conduct begin with a zero tolerance for gifts? How about lunch or dinner conducted for business purposes? A tray of holiday cookies? Free tickets to a sporting event or concert? A round of golf?

This is not just a theoretical issue but one that will be faced by most employees at some point in their career, as the following example illustrates:

It is your first day on the job and there is a cookie tray from a vendor saying, "Welcome." What do you do? Do you throw them out? Do you take them home? Do you tell your boss? Do you share them with your new coworkers? You decide to eat them. The next day you get your Standard of Conduct handbook, which specifically states that in your department no gifts, including edible gifts, can be accepted. This is not uncommon in certain business environments, in particular, those involving internal audit. Vendors send gifts all the time. In fact, it is how they do business. Also, it is common practice for companies to have individualized standards of conduct that have different levels of acceptable gifts. For example, some companies dictate that certain departments such as internal audit or purchasing may accept no gifts while other departments may accept gifts up to a certain value. These rules are arbitrary and vary from company to company. Getting back to our new employee, what does he do with the code of conduct he now has to sign? Well, there is no perfect answer. The point is that you should not put yourself in that situation.

The case for allowing some gifts is that a gratuity can be a gift provided by one party to another that does not involve or require a quid pro quo agreement, although the gift provider normally hopes for—if not expects—favorable treatment from the recipient of the gift. These types of gifts happen routinely in business. Most are harmless, such as business lunches, even though provided to ingratiate employees. The case against gratuities is that they cease being harmless when employees, either intentionally or subconsciously, begin to favor the gift giver. When that happens, even a minor act of favoritism meets the definition of fraud.

Proponents of gratuities argue that the recipients have done or will do nothing extraordinary to earn any gifts received and feel no obligation to respond in any way to the giver. When questioned, recipients usually reply indignantly that their integrity precludes them from being influenced by gratuities. Those who oppose the acceptance of gratuities from outsiders argue that, as a practical matter, human beings are motivated by rewards and either consciously or subconsciously will favor the gift giver where they must choose. Who would argue that, in a competitive business environment, the company that takes a purchasing agent to lunch at a fine restaurant is more likely to win a purchase order than the company that gives no gratuities? If the recipient of a gratuity is motivated to select products that are offered by the gratuity giver that are inferior to a competitor's, buy in excess of his or her employer's needs, or pay a price that is excessive, the employing entity is hurt as a result of the gratuity. In the end, the cost of gratuities given either increases the vendor's price or reduces his or her profits, and businesspeople are loath to reduce profits.

Many employers feel that gratuities are relatively harmless gifts, trivial in value, and not likely to influence their employees' judgment. However, what may appear trivial and noninfluencing to an employer may be regarded differently by the employees who receive them. Also, in many instances recipients come to expect gratuities provided by vendors on a recurring basis, and the employees are likely to favor those vendors in anticipation of gifts. Thus a presumptive sort of quid pro quo relationship develops.

To illustrate, an off-line general freight agent for the Southern Pacific Railroad was known to remark how he dreaded his monthly visit to a large fertilizer company's shipping department. His job was to visit Midwest manufacturers to sell them on shipping their products to West Coast destinations via Southern Pacific railways. The agent's visits, however, were an occasion that all 20 or so of the fertilizer company's employees looked forward to each month—a time when they were treated to an orgy of fine food and alcoholic beverages. Because all of the employees could not leave their worksite at once, they would arrange to go in two shifts. The railroad's agent had to accompany both shifts, and eat, drink, and make merry with them, and above all pick up the sizable check. He often complained about the ritual, explaining that Southern Pacific had attempted on several occasions to eliminate or cut back on it. However, whenever he missed a monthly orgy, he noticed a corresponding precipitous drop in the tonnage of fertilizer products shipped over Southern Pacific's tracks in the following month. Shipments were diverted to competing railroads. The agent presumed that competing railroads were not excepted from the monthly ritual. That is, any failures to take the gang out for a gala party each month would result in a very noticeable loss of fertilizer tonnage shipped. Gratuities that had begun innocently eventually had reached the level of extortion.

Set Clear Limits on Gratuities

If there are compelling reasons for allowing vendors and contractors to give gifts to employees, the reasons should be evaluated relative to the consequences and gratuities should be allowed as deemed appropriate. In all cases where it is decided to allow gratuities, limits should be imposed. All gratuity limits must be arbitrary because the level of influence resulting from a gratuity varies based on an individual's income level, position within the company, and so forth. For example, a clerk earning $25,000 may be influenced by a $200 gift while the president of the company may be influenced by a Caribbean cruise, therefore the code of conduct should be specific on the allowable dollar value.

Some entities limit the cumulative gratuities an employee may accept in a year to a specified amount, perhaps $300 or $500. In organizations where employees are allowed to accept gratuities, some companies require that they report what was accepted. Regardless, whatever standards are set by an entity, they should be explicit with regard to the sort and value of gifts that may be accepted by employees in the conduct of their employment and, more important, what cannot be accepted.

Case Study—Be Tuned In to Ethical Standards

Jane Smith, a Purchasing Agent for XYZ Company, received a television set from Contractor ABC, an outside vendor. There was no discussion between Ms. Smith and Contractor ABC that Ms. Smith would give the contractor preferential treatment.

The mere fact that Ms. Smith received an expensive new television set from a vendor shortly before the vendor received a $50,000 order from Ms. Smith does not necessarily mean that there was a quid pro quo agreement between the two parties. The vendor could successfully argue that the television set was a unilateral gift in expression of his gratitude and a generally accepted practice in his industry. If prosecuted, Jane Smith could argue that there was no fraud because there was no connection between the new television set and the $50,000 order she wrote to the vendor. If her employer did not prohibit the acceptance of such gifts, she had no reason not to accept it.

In such a case, an employer's code of conduct establishes a standard with regard to what kinds of gifts an employee may not accept from an outsider. In this instance, had the employer published standards of conduct that prohibited the acceptance of gifts such as the television set, Ms. Smith would have been prohibited from freely accepting the set and very likely would not have been motivated to write the $50,000 order that was not in her employer's best interests. Had such a standard existed, and had Ms. Smith written the order regardless, she would have been in clear violation of it, and the quid pro quo would have been much more easily demonstrated.

Answer These Questions Before You Write
Your Code of Conduct

- What entity interests would be served if vendors and others that we do business with were allowed to give gifts to our employees?

- In those instances where gratuities are deemed advantageous to the conduct of entity business—such as the provision of a meal as a convenience—should there be limitations? Should reciprocation be necessary to offset the gratuity? Will reciprocation be an allowable entity expense item? Should value limitations be required? If so, how? Per meal? Annually?

- What is considered a gift? Airline frequent flier miles? Candy? Flowers? Expense-paid trips? Tickets to sporting events? Anything of value?

- What are the possible consequences of not allowing gifts? Of allowing gifts without limitation? If gifts are to be limited, what type of limitations? Dollar amount?

- If gifts are allowed, should employees be required to disclose the gifts?

- Should some employees be subject to greater gift restrictions? For example, some companies restrict gifts to employees with the authority to award contracts or make purchasing decisions. Some companies severely restrict gifts that can be received by members of the internal auditing department.

- What disciplinary actions would be appropriate for violations of standards of conduct?

Ethics Officer

Entities considering the adoption of codes of conduct should appoint an ethics officer whose task it is to oversee the adequacy of the entity's ethics programs and to monitor compliance with them. Depending on the size of the entity, the ethics officer may be appointed to a full- or a part-time position. The ethics officer and staff should consider formal training in ethics matters and joining professional ethics organizations to share ideas and benefit from association with ethics officers from other entities. One professional association exclusively for managers of ethics, compliance, and business conduct programs, the "Business Ethics" website (www.web-miner.com/busethics.htm), lists articles and publications on the topics of business ethics, sample codes of conduct, and professional associations.

NOTES

1. *Encyclopedia Britannica* online, www.britannica.com.
2. www.thefreedictionary.com.
3. AICPA *Code of Professional Conduct*, www.aicpa.org.
4. *AICPA Professional Ethics Executive Committee Fact Sheet 2002–2003*, www.aicpa.org/download/ethics/ethics-committee-fact-sheet.pdf.
5. Sarbanes-Oxley Act of 2002; Section 406(a).
6. www.hierosgamos.org/articles/article-147-html. See link: www.Hayes Boone.com—'Knowledge Connect'—1/24/03—SEC Adopts Code of Ethics Disclosure Rules.
7. The Joint Ethics Enforcement Program (JEEP). http://ftp.aicpa.org /public/download/members/div/ethics/jeepcond-2.pdf.
8. *American Heritage Dictionary*, Second College Ed. (Boston: Houghton Mifflin Company, 1985).

10

EVIDENCE

Evidence is crucial to a successful investigation. The search for it in order to prove the fraud is the essence of an investigation. For most investigations, where fraud is discovered—or at least where fraud is strongly suspected—sufficient evidence to ensure a successful claim or conviction for fraud is usually the deciding factor on whether to proceed. Unfortunately, many people who are not adequately trained in fraud-specific investigations fail to understand the vital importance of evidence. Prosecution on the cases they develop often is declined, even though they are confident of their findings of fraud and may, in fact, be correct. It is evidence that transcends the gap between the investigator's firsthand knowledge of case circumstances and that which is conveyed to a judge or jury.

A wise man proportions his belief to the evidence.[1]

Many people tend to develop the consequences of fraud, such as the amount of the theft. However, when it comes down to naming the people involved, they fall short unless they have at least rudimentary training in the nature of evidence. So, good investigators must ask the following questions: Is there not sufficient additional evidence to be detected? Are investigators not sufficiently proactive or skilled to detect it? Both answers undoubtedly account for the failure of fraud cases discovered to advance to a stage where they are fully documented and ready for prosecution.

Many perpetrators are very clever and leave few if any clues. In these instances, the most skilled and proactive of investigators are challenged to detect recognizable evidence of fraud. However, the vast majority are not skilled in fraud detection and do not have sufficient knowledge of what evidence is required for fulfillment purposes. As a result, many potential fraud cases that could have advanced to prosecution do not. Accordingly, it follows that people who are better trained to recognize and gather relevant evidence could increase the number of fraud crimes that move forward to full discovery and perhaps prosecution.

The aim of this chapter is to sensitize investigators to the absolute necessity of making the discovery and development of evidence a primary objective. It provides readers with an awareness of the relevance of evidence in fraud investigations and a rudimentary understanding of the nature and importance of evidence. Only one caveat is offered. The author is an experienced fraud investigator, who has worked with (and against) prosecutors, but is not a prosecutor. Questions involving legal matters with regard to actual investigations in progress should be referred to an experienced prosecutor for authoritative answers. For investigative and legal content of a more definitive nature written by subject specialists, readers are referred to the *Accountant's Guide to Fraud Detection and Control.*[2]

The evidence collected in fraud-specific investigations falls into one of two groups: indicative evidence and validating evidence. Indicative evidence is always the object of the search during the proactive stage of the investigation.

INDICATIVE EVIDENCE

Indicative evidence by definition tends to indicate that fraud may have occurred, but it does not prove it. During the proactive stage of fraud-specific investigations, you are looking for indications that fraud may have occurred without having the benefit of any evidence of any kind that it in fact has. In this stage, there is little guidance in the methods to use and few indications to suggest what sort of fraud to look for. Experience and intuition are the only main-stays. In this proactive stage, the main quest is not necessarily to find fraud, fraud perpetrators, or assemble evidence to prosecute them. That will come later. Rather, the less experienced merely sift through large amounts of raw data looking for leads or indications that fraud may have occurred. The first sighting of fraud is usually found in evidence traces that in themselves do little to suggest fraud. The traces first must be recognized as indicia of fraud and must be seen as a preliminary sign of a fraud determination. Inexperience may lead to overlooking evidence traces and failing to see their fraud potential.

To illustrate, there was an instance when an investigator who had been examining payments for contract building maintenance services totally missed seeing the fraud potential in indicative evidence he had detected. In the process of examining a payment of about $5,000 for cleaning window blinds in a large building, he noticed that the vendor had failed to deduct a discount of about 25 percent, which had been negotiated as a contract term. The contractor's invoice, when presented, requested payment for $5,000—the open market price advertised for the contractor's services. However, the invoice failed to make any mention of the 25 percent discount or to deduct it from the amount due. The $5,000 amount was approved by the company's representative and paid in full. Had the 25 percent discount been applied, the amount claimed and paid should have been $3,750. The reviewer in this case felt the overcharge was a simple clerical error. However, experienced fraud-sensitive investigators would have raised a red flag and wondered if there was any reason to suspect the transaction. That is, they would have asked themselves these questions: "Is it reasonable for a competent person not to remember the very significant terms of the contract he or she participated in and/or very likely negotiated?" "Could the failure to deduct the $1,250 discount be more than a mere oversight?" "Was it a simple case of negligence by the contractor and the victim's representative, or was it fraud?" It could have been either.

Readers also should ask what they themselves would have done in this case.

In the actual case from which this example was drawn, the reviewer was not sensitive to fraud, was not aware of the red flags of fraud, and was not suspicious of the transaction. Acting like most inexperienced internal auditors, he proudly reported his finding to operating personnel, who took prompt action to recover the overpayment. Many reviewers are sensitive of a need to justify their work by reporting opportunities to save their client or employer money. Experienced fraud-sensitive reviewers would suspect that they had discovered a possible indication of fraud. Had the reviewer recognized this possibility, he would have quietly noted his observation in his work papers without calling it to anyone's attention or showing any outward indication of his discovery. He then could have chosen to validate his discovery immediately or at a more opportune time. Actually, there would be nothing lost in delaying reporting his discovery of the overcharge and obtaining the $1,250 refund. If the overpayment was later found to be merely an oversight by the contracting officer, it could always be recovered then.

To validate his discovery, the reviewer should have assumed the attitude that if his discovery involved fraud, it is likely that it happened before and involved either one of or both parties. Accordingly, he should have examined other contracts and/or delivery orders completed by that contractor, and/or other contract transactions involving the same employee. If they were indeed dishonest, it is a good possibility that other similar transactions could be identified. Each additional questionable transaction discovered would irreparably damage any plausibility excuse that the accused might offer and would more clearly establish that there was intent to defraud.

VALIDATING EVIDENCE

Once indicative evidence pointing to possible fraud has been discovered, the object of the search shifts to validating evidence. Validating evidence is anything that confirms the indicative evidence. Once this confirmation has been made, the sum of the indicative evidence gathered may be properly described as evidence. Incidentally, the terms indicative evidence and validating evidence are used here to clarify the progression of a proactive fraud-specific investigation from the zero evidence stage through the point where bona fide evidence is developed and the reactive stage of fraud-specific auditing begins.

The initial search for indicative evidence clearly begins in the proactive stage, which involves a search for anything that indicates the possibility of fraud. Technically speaking, indicative evidence is not evidence per se, in that nothing can be concluded from it. Proactive examination continues until one is able to conclude that fraud has in fact been detected. Once this point is reached (personal judgment) the investigation becomes reactive. In the reactive stage, objectives shift to searching for validating or corroborating evidence to either firm up the proactive discovery or negate it.

Indicative evidence can take any form and you must examine it with what might be called a controlled state of paranoia—that is, you must suspect everything. In more technical terms, you are exercising professional skepticism, which is talked about earlier in this book, in reference to external auditors and SAS 99.

Often, losses due to fraud are noticed before there is any discovery of evidence to conclude whether the losses are due to fraud or waste. In such instances, with no evidence to indicate that fraud was involved, the losses are usually attributed to waste resulting from someone's negligence or incompetence. It is not until sufficient evidence of fraud has been detected (if indeed it is ever sought) that the losses are attributed to fraud, and most entities experiencing losses rarely look for evidence of fraud, or have historically had the capability to look for fraud. Many, if they were to employ a fraud specific investigator, would be surprised to find that fraud was the real culprit. Experienced investigators usually begin their work with the mind-set that long-standing employees have the intelligence to not waste assets, and look for the fraud angle in their actions. Take note: Evidence is the determining factor in classifying losses as waste or fraud, and entities do not find evidence of fraud if they do not look for it.

Experience is a key ingredient for making a case and getting the evidence, as noted by the following case.

CASE 10.1   The Borrowed Assets

John Doe falsified various accounting documents on July 1, obtaining $100,000 of his employer's funds to invest in the stock market. Using the $100,000, he bought stock on July 6, intending to repay his employer out of his profits. John was lucky. He sold his stock for $200,000 on July 9 and promptly replaced the funds he had taken without his employer's knowledge. However, the falsified documents were discovered on July 10, and John was accused of defrauding his employer. There was never any question that John falsified the documents and received the $100,000. When interrogated, he admitted everything and stated that he invested the proceeds in the stock market. The employer is outraged, and wishes to prosecute John for fraud.

Is it likely that John Doe will be prosecuted based on the evidence given in this scenario? If so, is it likely that he will be found guilty of fraud? The answers are no, and no. The evidence provided here does not establish that John intended to steal the $100,000. Nor does it show that the employer was harmed. At trial, John would be likely to argue that he only intended to borrow the money for a few days. He is willing to pay the employer interest. He will say that his investment was based on a dependable tip and will argue that his replacement of the money on July 9, before it ever was discovered missing, is proof of his claim. John's act was outrageous and illegal, and he may be disciplined by his employer; but it could be difficult to convict him of fraud.

In a real-life situation however, involving trained and experienced fraud investigators, the case would very likely include more evidence than was presented in Case 10.1. Most of us would likely recognize John as a thief and use procedures designed to prove it, if at all possible. To begin with, he falsified documents. Although there is a first time for everything, on many occasions it is not the person's first offense. It is only when they are not caught and get bigger and bolder that things go wrong for them. John may have borrowed money from his employer on prior occasions—this is a trail you need to pursue. You would have to assume that John could not possibly have been so lucky in all his prior stock market investments or possible other gambling episodes. By documenting the other occasions, if they indeed exist, some of which John very likely did not repay, you would then have shown other instances of John's intention to risk his employer's funds. Had other examples been provided, John would have been prosecuted and very likely convicted.

In my experience, fraudsters' rationalizations when confronted are very interesting:

> "I'm just borrowing the funds."
>
> "I deserve it—I'm underpaid."
>
> "I worked overtime but didn't get paid for it."
>
> "I should have been promoted by now."
>
> "I'm not hurting anyone."
>
> "Everyone else is doing it."

Obviously, the first comment applies in the previous example to John Doe—perhaps he feels his repayment to the company vindicates him. However, what if he lost the money on the stock market? Would he have "borrowed" more to try and get it back? Would he then be in a loop from which he could never exit?

To illustrate uncertainties in prosecution actions, even when the evidence appears to be compelling, consider the next case. It involved apparent fraudulent acts by a government contractor and his subsequent prosecution in a federal district court. Under the contract, the contractor was responsible for repairing government equipment, such as mobile aircraft electrical generators, shipped to him by military bases.

CASE 10.2   Equipment Repair Contractor's False Claims

The contract was a time and material (T & M) contract. That is, it provided that the contractor would be reimbursed on the basis of the number of direct labor hours he expended on equipment repaired at a fixed hourly rate as specified in the contract. He also would be reimbursed for the actual cost of repair parts purchased. The fixed hourly rate had been bid by the contractor in competition against other contractors and normally would include his average cost of an hour of direct labor, his prorated hourly overhead and administrative costs, and profit applicable to those costs. For example, assuming that the contractor spent 100 direct labor hours to repair an item of equipment at a contract hourly rate of $30, and had purchased $500 of repair parts, he would invoice the government $3,500 (100 hours × $30 + $500 = $3,500).

The contract also required that the contractor make his records available for audit, should it be requested. It was. The audit disclosed he had falsely inflated the labor hours he claimed to have expended and had falsely claimed the purchase of repair parts. The fraud was so blatant, for example, that addresses given for many of the parts suppliers were vacant lots.

Also, as clearly proved in an audit of payroll records, the hours charged to the job by the employees alleged to have worked on it had far exceeded the total weekly hours that the employees named had worked and been paid for.

Armed with seemingly indisputable evidence of fraud, the contractor was indicted, prosecuted, and convicted of fraud in federal court. What is particularly noteworthy in this instance, however, were the somewhat angry after trial comments of the assistant U.S. attorney who prosecuted the case. He complained to the auditors that he had difficulty convincing the jury of the contractor's guilt and had come close to failing. Next time, he advised them, "Give me stronger evidence of the contractor's 'intent' to defraud the government." What he was looking for, if possible, was evidence that the contractor had committed fraud on more than this one contract, thereby making it clear that he had fraudulent intent and that he was, in fact, a criminal.

In this case, the auditors believed there was compelling evidence of the contractor's guilt. However, the contractor's defense attorney raised a question as to whether the contractor was in fact a criminal, pleading that one apparent crime does not a criminal make. If there was no other evidence of criminal conduct, perhaps this was just a careless bookkeeping error.

This contractor's guilt later appeared to be certain when viewed in the context of a corollary case that involved a U.S. Air Force sergeant who was allegedly in collusion with the contractor. The sergeant was to be tried separately by a military court for sending perfectly serviceable generators, not in need of repair, to the contractor, who merely stored them for a short time before returning them and billing the government for work not done. The contractor allegedly split the proceeds with the sergeant.

Evidence is literally the heart of a fraud-specific investigation. Find as much of it as possible, corroborate it, and document, document, document!

NOTES

1. David Hume, British philosopher, 1711–1776; http://academics.vmi.edu /psy_dr/Hume%20on%20miracles.htm.

2. Howard R. Davia, Patrick C. Coggins, John C. Wideman, and Joseph T. Kastantin, *Accountant's Guide to Fraud Detection and Control*, (New York: John Wiley & Sons, 2000).

11

SYMPTOMATIC FRAUD INVESTIGATION

One of the most difficult things about proactive investigations is that they require people to institute search procedures to detect fraud where there is no evidence per se that fraud may exist. Performing proactive procedures is much more difficult than performing reactive procedures, which begin with solid leads. One problem is that indicia of fraud committed by cautious and/or expert perpetrators are rarely found without initiating relatively blind search procedures. Without that initial finding of indicia of fraud, reactive investigations never occur. The best perpetrators tend to be cautious and conservative in their criminal endeavors, leaving little if anything to be detected. Luckily for their victims, not all fraud perpetrators are ultra cautious and their crimes leave faint traces that can be detected by enlightened investigators.

In many cases, those traces are bona fide evidence that directly indicates fraud may have occurred and those traces can eventually be used as evidentiary material. However, in many other cases the traces—which cannot be characterized as evidence—can be better described as the symptoms or effects of the crime. Rather than having to resort to random or intuitive searches in the hope of detecting scant bits of evidence upon which to build more substantive examinations, you are advised first to search for these effects or symptoms to enhance further efforts. This practice is called symptomatic fraud investigation. For the record, a symptom is defined as a circumstance or phenomenon regarded as an indication or characteristic of a condition or event.[1]

Accordingly, when practicing symptomatic fraud investigations, you should take note of circumstances or events that could be fraud and initiate procedures as if the circumstances or events were indicia of fraud. Note that the circumstances or events referred to are not evidence of fraud but may be symptoms of fraud.

Most observers will not regard these symptoms as suspicious— nor are they necessarily. In most instances, they are merely the result of innocent events. However, not infrequently, the symptoms, when properly interpreted, are indications of fraud. The mind-set of the interpreter affects how these symptoms are interpreted. Those people who have confidence in their fellow humans not to steal from them will view the symptoms with concern rather than suspicion. However, good fraud investigators must cultivate an attitude of controlled paranoia or skepticism, recognizing fraud possibilities in what others may regard as regrettable but normal events.

Sometimes paranoia's just having all the facts.[2]

For example, consider a leaking warehouse roof that had been replaced within the last two or three years. How should the leak be regarded? Was the contractor who replaced the roof (1) innocent of any liability? (2) negligent? (3) guilty of fraud? or (4) none of the above? Conceivably, the correct answer could be any one or more of these four choices. If the contractor replaced the roof in full accord with the contract specifications, neither choice (2), (3), or (4) would be appropriate. If the new roof was damaged after the contractor finished the job, and water was able to penetrate the damaged surface, choice (1) is correct, all but ruling out choices (2) through (4).

However, if the contractor deviated from contract specifications for the job, perhaps substituting cheaper materials or cutting corners to save costs, then choice (3) is correct. Hence, the symptom of a leaking roof can in an extreme instance lead to the discovery of fraud—in this case, defective delivery fraud. Accordingly, in seeking fraud you are well advised to look to events and circumstances that may exhibit the effects of fraud. These might be gleaned from an entity's formal as well as informal complaint registry system. This is especially true in today's environment due to the recent creation of the anonymous whistleblower hotlines, resulting from many well-publicized corporate frauds and the Sarbanes-Oxley legislation. The minutes or memoranda of all meetings should be carefully monitored to detect complaints, performance deviations, and the like. Nonroutine and all emergency spending outlays may harbor fraud possibilities. Examiners should bear in mind that asset theft fraud involves a loss of assets that should leave discernable traces.

From the point of view of the financial statement auditor, the AICPA's SAS 99, "Consideration of Fraud in a Financial Statement Audit" (discussed in Chapter 2 in this book), attempts to establish standards and provide guidance to auditors with respect to fraud. It requires external auditors to become proactive. SAS 99 stresses professional skepticism, requires planning for the possibility of fraud, and requires a written assessment of fraud risks. With this pronouncement, the accounting profession is attempting to transform the external auditor from reactive to proactive as it relates to financial statement fraud.

SYMPTOMS OF FRAUD

A defective delivery of goods or services is perhaps one of the well-known fraud symptoms. Recipients of goods or services that are defective tend to complain. Accordingly, before electing to search for defective delivery fraud and beginning an examination by selecting random payment transactions involving the acquisition of goods or services, you may choose to begin by determining whether there are any complaints, formal or informal, regarding inferior quality of products or workmanship.

In an interesting case, a fraud was discovered somewhat by chance, by examiners searching for defective delivery fraud. At least they were focusing on one particular type of fraud; however, it is quite likely that it could have been discovered had they engaged in symptomatic auditing. In a random selection of payment transactions, the examiners chose payment for about $5,000 made to recondition a water storage tank (see the case example in Chapter 6) located on the roof of a high-rise office building. Upon inspecting the supposedly reconditioned tank, they discovered a shell fraud—absolutely no work had been done. The walls of the water-filled tank were encrusted with extensive rust and scale.

The point of this illustration is that because the water tank was badly corroded, as reported by the inspecting engineer, it is quite likely the water quality was also bad. It is also likely that users had complained of polluted water. If they had, a review of the complaints, together with the tank's maintenance history, would likely have found the tank supposedly had been reconditioned recently. With that information in mind, they would have had good reason to question if the tank had, in fact, been reconditioned. An inspection similar to the one made by chance would have revealed the fraud.

In an illustration of a fraud discovered via symptoms, an office suite complained of persistent water leaks originating from their ceiling. A parking area was located over the office suite, and eventually the leaks were traced to water that had somehow penetrated from the parking area. This was not an unusual event, given the circumstances, except for the fact the parking area recently had been extensively resurfaced, and the contractor had been required to install an extremely durable and dependably waterproof rubber-like membrane. There appeared to be three possibilities to explain the leaks. The rubber-like material may have been defective; the membrane was applied improperly; or the contractor did not install the membrane as was required by the contract.

Here is what was interesting. Normally, when a situation such as this occurs, the contracting entity complains to the installing contractor and requires that the leak be fixed. In many cases, the leak would never be fixed adequately, and the problem would never be resolved satisfactorily. However, if a paranoid, fraud-minded examiner were made aware of the leak, he or she would have likely suspected faulty performance by the contractor and would have arranged to test the parking lot surface to determine if the resurfacing job was performed in accordance with contract specifications. This is what actually happened, and the examiner discovered that the contractor had failed to install the rubber-like membrane that was specified by the contract, installing a cheaper substitute instead. It was also discovered that the contractor had not done this by error, but with the deliberate intent of defrauding his customer.

VARIATIONS IN ACTUAL VERSUS PLANNED COST

Variations in actual versus planned cost sometimes reveal symptoms of fraud, that is, unexplained differences between planned versus actual costs. Companies, particularly the more sophisticated ones, spend a lot of time and effort creating budgets and projections. These budgets are used as a tool to assess a company's performance as compared to what was expected. Stock prices, bonuses, and the like are determined based on actual versus planned results. So management should be able to provide detailed explanations as to why they outperformed or underperformed compared to budget. Incomplete or sketchy justification for these potential symptomatic variances, if investigated, could uncover fraud. Also, many frauds have been discovered when variances are not discussed or managers promise to provide information "at a later date," but never actually provide a satisfactory explanation. Follow up is a key ingredient.

CASE 11.1   Driving a Hard Bargain

An automobile rental entity became concerned when its automobile capital costs had risen significantly over the expected amounts, but was at a loss to explain the increases other than to speculate that the vehicles were receiving hard usage. The internal auditor who was assigned to investigate the anomaly discovered that fraud may have been the underlying reason when she discovered the following events:

To maintain its automotive fleet properly, the entity involved had contracted with a service company to perform its vehicular maintenance needs as they arose. The contract called for the repair and replacement of necessary parts and components. However, the contractor was also instructed to limit repairs to those vehicles that were economically repairable, factoring in the age of each vehicle and the estimated cost of repair. He was instructed to identify those vehicles that were not economically reparable and those would be subsequently sold at periodic auctions conducted by the entity. The internal auditor, however, was one of those paranoid types that are not easily fooled. She discovered that the service contractor was designating easily reparable vehicles as not economically reparable. Then, when the vehicles were sold at auction, the service contractor's agents knew which vehicles were in excellent condition and were able to acquire them at prices only slightly above those of vehicles in poor condition.

When companies operate on cash-based accounting, their primary financial management objectives are often on spending in accordance with cash availability, rather than spending to meet operating needs. Accordingly, rarely are there notable differences between financial plans and actual expenditures in year-end operating reports. For example, if budget account #12345 plans for the expenditure of $12,568, it is extremely likely that actual costs will be within 1 percent of that amount. That is because managers often learn to quickly spend everything they are given to spend, or be censured for not meeting their spending goals. It is not unusual for managers in cash basis environments not to seek the best prices when forced to use up their year-end surpluses. Likewise, clever fraud perpetrators in these cash basis environments are aware of the spending goals and frequently "help" embattled managers by stealing a portion of their year-end surpluses.

CASE 11.2   The Surplus Funds Account

A 33-year-old woman was sentenced to 18 months in prison for embezzling $395,991 from a branch of the Interior Department where she worked. She was also ordered to pay full restitution. The embezzlement occurred on 46 occasions over a two-year period. It was not explained how the discovery occurred.

This case is particularly relevant in discussing symptomatic examinations in that the vagaries of the fiscal systems in use suggest a viable avenue for proactive fraud examination. It was determined that the woman embezzled the funds from what are known in government circles as "expiring fiscal year appropriations." Any entity operating under the cash basis of accounting method is vulnerable to the same fraud. This includes government entities at all levels, most colleges and universities, not-for-profit entities, and the like. They receive their annual operating funds from a funding agency, such as the U.S. Congress, or a state legislature, and their use of the funds is limited to a specific fiscal year. Funds not used at the end of the year may not legally be used in subsequent years.

The perpetrator in this case observed that the federal agency involved ended their fiscal years with large unspent appropriation balances, and she took note of the fact the status of those unspent funds was never reviewed. Accordingly, she saw the opportunity to embezzle portions of the unspent balances each year, unnoticed, without generating any complaints from the departments involved. The point of this case is that unspent balances that remain unspent at the end of fiscal periods is a symptom of the opportunity for fraud.[3]

Fraud investigators working in organizations employing cash basis accounting systems, however, can be as clever as perpetrators by focusing examinations on transactions occurring near but before the close of fiscal periods. The symptoms to look for are surges in spending in the last two months of the fiscal year. This extraordinary spending activity can mask the work of a fraud perpetrator seeking to tap the entity's unspent money. Experience has shown that some corporate managers tend to defer discretionary spending until the end of their fiscal year, at which time they can be confident of how much cash remains available to be spent. Accordingly, the fraud perpetrator who acts just before the start of an entity's shopping spree at the end of a fiscal year often has a wide choice of available fund pools to locate his or her fraud scheme.

There are many illustrations of bad financial management in cash-based organizations. Consider the case of the university employee (see the case study in Chapter 1) who was discovered to have created $149,190 in payroll checks for nonexistent employees over a six-year period, cashed the checks, and pocketed the money. Despite the loss of these sums to fraud, the university obviously had no suspicions that she was a thief when it awarded her the President's Award in 1996 as the university's most valued employee.

She became a suspect only after her husband was suspected in an unrelated stolen check crime and U.S. Postal Inspectors searching their home found university payroll stubs under different names and became suspicious. In another instance, a federal government employee, using a government credit card, was accidentally discovered to have purchased several hundred thousand dollars' worth of camera film over a period of a year or so, which he resold for cash to finance a drug habit. His crime was discovered when the seller of the film became suspicious of the large purchases and alerted the buyer's employer. The cash basis federal agency involved had no prior suspicions that its employee was engaged in a theft of such significance.

"SHOULD COST" APPROACH

From time to time, fraud examiners speak of a "should cost" approach to fraud investigations. Basically this means that when examining a service or product that has been delivered, you should make an attempt to determine whether the price paid is reasonable—that is, what should it cost? The unit price charged for the product or service delivered is, in effect, the symptom of a possible fraud. If the price paid seems to be too high, procedures should be initiated to determine how the price was established and to verify whether it really was too high. If it indeed was too high, you should initiate a fraud-specific examination to determine if someone was culpable, who that person is, and if indeed it was fraud.

Many frauds are enabled by conspiracies that exist between contractors or vendors and key entity employees, wherein the employee—in return for a kickback or other profit-sharing arrangement—takes the necessary steps to direct the contract to his or her conspirator, aware that the price is higher than the best prevailing market price. The contractor or vendor charges more for the product or service to be delivered in order to pay for the employee's kickback. The excessive price paid is the cost of the fraud to the victim.

People who specialize in should-cost auditing are very good at sensing whether their employers paid too much for a product or service. Such was the case of an internal auditor who was examining purchases of office equipment when he came across a large order for calculators. The unit price charged to his employer troubled him, for it appeared about $100 too high per item. During his lunch hour, he decided to check out the market rate for the calculators and visited an office supply store a few blocks away from his employer's site. After inquiring about the sales price for an identical calculator, his suspicions were proven. The merchant would have sold him one of the same calculators for about $100 less than his employer was paying for several dozen of them. The auditor's examination from that point on became a fraud-specific audit as there could have been no other logical explanation for such behavior.

EMPLOYEE LIFESTYLE CHANGES

Often referred to as one of the key red flags of fraud, when employees profit from fraud, their lifestyles improve dramatically. Although many people find it objectionable to target individuals for fraud-specific investigations when there is no evidence that they committed fraud, doing so can be very productive in disclosing fraud. Of course, any reviews of this nature must be conducted with the utmost discretion, and any information disclosed must be kept very confidential. The best question to ask an audience eager to conduct this type of examination is: "What if you are wrong?"

Under the theory that people commit fraud because they have a need, they are greedy, the opportunity exists for them to steal, and they have a low expectation of being caught, they sometimes get carried away with their ill-gotten gains. In the case of the negligent internal control clerk in Chapter 4, the fraudster began to spend money far beyond his salary level. He would take fellow workers to lunch at trendy, expensive restaurants. He stated that an aunt had died and left him her fortune. Of course, no one questioned his story, until one particular day. By accident, it was discovered that he had submitted false invoices for building maintenance projects and collected the payments. The theft exceeded $900,000. With the new employee hotlines, it is possible someone could have noticed his lavish spending and reported it to his employer. However, investigators must remain impartial and must be careful not to fall prey to a vindictive, possibly jealous coworker. Nonetheless, knowing the red flags of fraud may have alerted senior personnel at an earlier stage.

Red Flags

A red flag is an irregularity that may relate to time, frequency, place, amount, or personality. While this concept could be applied to most of the areas discussed in this book, employee theft is one of the areas where it is sometimes the most relevant. Business red flags include overrides of normal controls by management and/or officers, irregular or poorly explained management activities, problems or delays in getting requested information, and significant or unusual changes in customers or suppliers. Business red flags also include transactions that lack documentation or normal approval, employees hand-delivering checks, customer complaints about delivery, poor computer file access controls, and poor password controls, among many others.

Personal red flags and those which feed a skeptical mind when conducting a lifestyle review include living beyond one's means; dissatisfaction with the job conveyed to fellow employees; unusually close association with suppliers; severe personal financial losses; addiction to drugs, alcohol or gambling; change in personal circumstances; and outside business interests. In addition, there are employees who consistently rationalize poor performance, see beating the system as an intellectual challenge, provide unreliable communications and reports, and rarely take vacations or sick time.

While none of these individually mean that an employee is committing fraud, their existence should heighten awareness. A combination of these factors would obviously raise such level of awareness and possibly prompt inquiries.

Picture the couple who (as noted in Chapter 1 of this book) earned a collective $69,000 a year but had a home with a swimming pool, hot tub, and a four-car garage, as well as a second home with eight bedrooms and a six-car garage, on the waterfront, worth $800,000. Anything wrong with this lifestyle? They also owned an island cottage, eight cars, two trucks, two boats, three jet skis, a doll collection worth $170,000 and had $85,000 of recently purchased U.S. Savings Bonds. They paid private college tuition for two sons and gave substantial amounts to family members. Anything wrong with this lifestyle?

They pled guilty to embezzling $3.28 million from a union. The wife inflated and diverted automatic payroll deductions destined for a credit union to her own account. The fraud lasted for nine years without detection because she was responsible for reconciling the union accounts. The fraud was discovered accidentally when someone at the credit union became suspicious of large sums of money moving in and out of union accounts.

A kleptomaniac is someone who helps himself, because he can't help himself.[4]

NOTES

1. *American Heritage Dictionary*, Second College Ed. (Boston: Houghton Mifflin Company, 1985).

2. William S. Burroughs, author, 1914–1997; http://www.allthingswilliam .com/health.html.

3. Compiled from various staff writer reports, Associated Press, "Crime and Justice/Virginia," *Washington Post*, May 16, 2000.

4. Henry Morgan, buccaneer, 1635–1688; http://www.worldofquotes.com /author/Henry-Morgan/1/.

12

FRAUD INVESTIGATION ALTERNATIVES

Let there be no mistake—detecting fraud is difficult. Fraud investigators must utilize every opportunity to maximize fraud detection and prevention. They must be resourceful and innovative. Creative and imaginative. To that end, certain alternatives to the direct proactive fraud-specific investigative techniques discussed throughout this text can be used to combat fraud. Surprisingly, in some instances that alternative is to do nothing. Remember the question posed in Chapter 11: What if you are wrong?

MONITORING KNOWN OR SUSPECTED FRAUD

From time to time fraud is detected that you have reason to suspect may exist to an extent far beyond that which you have discovered. When it is detected, four questions (among many others) need to be answered:

1. Do we keep looking until we have found it all, or most of it?
2. Do we recommend internal controls designed to limit further occurrences of it?
3. Is a processing system change justified?
4. Do we do nothing?

In question 1, if the fraud is too difficult to detect and may require an inordinate amount of investigative effort, further examination may not be a viable option. For example, if the expenditure of resources is in excess of the likely cost of the fraud being perpetrated, then conducting unlimited research may not be a prudent decision. Of course, defining the cost of the fraud is a somewhat difficult calculation to begin with.

Option 2 is sometimes a viable alternative provided that suitable internal controls can be devised that are effective as well as cost beneficial and assuming they do not unduly suppress productivity. Accordingly, internal controls may or may not be a viable alternative. In a public company setting, the decision is more skewed. For public companies, the existence and testing of internal controls is now required under Sarbanes-Oxley and under the Public Company Accounting Oversight Board's Auditing Standard No. 2, "An Audit of Internal Control Over Financial Reporting Performed in Conjunction with an Audit of Financial Statements."

Cost/benefit studies are necessary in order to fully evaluate option 3. Changes, particularly in large sophisticated systems, usually are not accomplished easily or cheaply. What about option 4? Are there circumstances where it would be prudent to do nothing to suppress or disclose fraud that it is believed will continue? The answer is yes.

The merits of considering doing nothing versus doing something are best illustrated by recalling a personal experience, as described in Case 12.1.

CASE 12.1   How Deep Should You Dig to Uncover Fraud?

A client discovered that their controller had been embezzling funds by writing manual checks to herself. The controller was fired for insubordination and begged to keep her job. No wonder—within a few days of being fired, the month-end bank statement arrived at the client's location.

The owner of the company saw three checks written to the controller, which upon closer inspection had been posted to bank loan accounts.

Historically, the bank statements were received at the client's location by the controller, who removed the manual checks from the bank statements before the owner received the package. Given the number of computer checks generated a month, together with a regular batch of manual checks, it was no surprise the owner would not have noticed the missing checks. The package was then given to the same controller to perform the bank reconciliation. While most of you are gasping that such a lack of control existed, it should be pointed out this was a family business and trust was implicit.

It should also be pointed out that this process has been effectively negated by the fact that banks, for the most part, no longer return actual canceled checks with statements, preferring to enclose sheets with copies of checks, several to a page, or provide a CD with check copies, or allow the customer to go online and view canceled checks.

Notwithstanding the facilities now available, the client was faced with a predicament. They knew for certain the controller had taken around $7,000. They had already fired her for another reason. How much had this person taken? She had been there six years. The business had been brisk for a while but they now had a large bank overdraft and their accountant told them they were spending too much on inventory.

The client had a fidelity bond with up to $500,000 of coverage. How much would it cost them to fully investigate the theft? How far back should they go? What if they refer it to the authorities and it hits the press? Would the customers think the company was in financial trouble? Also just as crucial—what if the vendors thought they would not be able to pay their bills?

These are the typical questions facing a business in this position. Especially a smaller business and especially a retail business, as in this case. After pondering the decision and meeting with counsel, they pressed forward. The additional work uncovered a fraud that went back five years and extended to over $600,000! By turning the case over to the authorities, the client was able to discover that the checks went directly into the controller's bank account. The evidence was overwhelming. There were copies of canceled checks paid to the controller; the backs of the checks contained the controller's endorsement and personal bank account numbers; a lifestyle review uncovered a substantial house, cars, and lavish parties on a salary of about $30,000, and a husband on disability. The fidelity bond carrier wrote a check for $500,000 and the controller got the better part of five years in jail. There was little publicity on the case and the client moved on to bigger and better things with their business.

For a short while, they had considered doing nothing but in this case, it was just as well they did something.

Many people find it disturbing that a fraud may be occurring and they have no ability to stop it. However vexing it may be, doing nothing is sometimes the most prudent decision. Nevertheless, the fraud should never be simply forgotten. It should be monitored regularly through sampling and the cost/benefit aspects of controlling it should be regularly recalculated. Many banks and retail stores find themselves in similar situations. Their audits of daily cash shortages occurring at teller windows and cash registers are sometimes so consistent that they are positive that cashiers are stealing petty amounts. Nevertheless, often they have no practical alternative other than to do nothing but monitor the shortages to ensure that they do not exceed tolerable limits.

MONITORING OPERATIONAL AREAS AT RISK OF FRAUD

Besides searching for evidence of fraud, entities often find it worthwhile to periodically evaluate operational systems that may be at risk of fraud. In their examinations they, in effect, place themselves in the role of a fraud perpetrator and attempt to devise schemes to evade internal controls and perpetrate fraud. In some instances, when they believe that a system can be penetrated, they actually test their theories by attempting to perpetrate the fraud envisioned, lacking only the intent to defraud the entities involved. Note: Any auditors who may be considering doing this are advised to take care to notify appropriate trustworthy individuals that a simulated fraud will be attempted.

In one government example, U.S. General Accounting Office (GAO) auditors examining an automated payroll system felt that a system weakness would allow payroll checks to be issued to nonexistent employees. To test their theory and to vividly demonstrate the impersonal aspect of computer-generated payroll checks, they successfully caused the system to issue phony checks to Disney cartoon characters such as Mickey Mouse and Donald Duck.

To correct such a situation, auditors normally first consider measures designed to close the weakness discovered, if that is feasible and cost beneficial. If not, then auditors are obliged to continue to perform test audits perpetually to ascertain the degree to which the payroll weakness is being exploited.

In a previous example, internal auditors examining a large supply control system detected what they considered to be a weakness that would allow fraud to occur. Anticipating that the mere reporting of the weakness would be contested by the organizational subentity responsible, they decided to test their theory. Using an unsecured computer, an auditor entered a purchase order into the supply control system, which in effect notified the automated supply system that a purchase order for about $96,000 had been issued for tool kits and was due in. The auditor assigned a fictitious stock number. Several weeks later the auditor, using the same unsecured computer, created a false receiving report notice that caused the supply system to record the receipt of the merchandise ordered and to update its inventories. The supplies ordered, of course, were never received. A few days later, the auditor mailed an invoice to the entity involved, requesting payment for the merchandise. The automated system, noting that it had all the required documentary evidence to make payment—a valid order, a notice of receipt of the merchandise, and an invoice requesting payment—caused a check to be issued to the fictitious vendor. A short time later another fictitious order was placed, and another check was issued.

The auditor was never able to determine that an actual fraud using the system weakness he had discovered had ever been exploited. Although it was suspected as a contributing cause of past inventory shortages, no proof was found. Nevertheless, something had to be done about the newly discovered weakness. The first recommendations involved improving internal controls, such as securing unattended computers and tightening password control. These controls, however, were considered insufficient to fully close the fraud opportunities noted because over 200 authorized users had to retain access to the system and hence would continue to have the opportunity to conduct the fraud described. The solution elected was to test supply acquisition transactions periodically to determine whether the system weaknesses had been exploited as well as to introduce an audit presence that would present a risk factor, even though minimal, into any fraud perpetration attempts.

FRAUD INVESTIGATIONS AND INTERNAL CONTROL

Aside from those internal controls that are designed primarily to ensure the integrity of an entity's accounting system, some internal controls are designed to be fraud specific. The objective of fraud-specific internal controls is to prevent or deter fraud. Internal auditors may recommend the imposition of fraud-specific internal controls as well as suggest design features.

The design and installation of internal control systems is rarely, if ever, a prime responsibility of an entity's internal auditors. This is appropriate, for the most part, for internal auditing tends to be a more or less adversarial activity. An entity's internal auditors, although not usually directly responsible for internal controls, are nevertheless responsible for periodically testing the suitability and efficacy of the internal controls in operation. Independent auditors, during their periodic annual audits, are clearly charged with the responsibility of determining that a client's internal control system does, in fact, assure that the client's accounting system does fully and accurately collect and report all financially relevant data. As stated earlier in this book, for public companies, the requirements of Sarbanes-Oxley and other new legislation have taken internal controls into a whole new realm.

Some internal auditors attempt to distance themselves from the design of internal controls, citing a need to maintain objectivity in their review and evaluation of those controls. And there is considerable support in favor of maintaining their objectivity. However, there are also valid arguments for involving internal auditors in the internal control evaluation and design process. Many internal auditors consider reliance on fraud-specific internal controls indispensable, due to the enormity of the fraud universe and the disadvantageous position they occupy in their battle with fraud perpetrators. In most organizations, and particularly in large and complex entities, fraud perpetrators have a clear advantage over fraud auditors in being able to select where and when to commit fraud. Unless they are totally inept—which few are—they can select target areas for fraud in which their advantage is maximized.

Conversely, internal auditors must endure the unenviable position of not knowing where or when fraud perpetrators are likely to strike and having too few resources to do justice to them all, or even a significant portion of them. The alternative is to resort to internal controls, which increase the risk of detection for fraud perpetrators and in so doing, deters them. Arguments for including auditors in the internal control design and evaluation process are likewise strong. They generally have a more comprehensive knowledge of an entity's management process than do financial accountants who customarily act as internal control system custodians and, given their experience in fraud and error detection, they are well prepared to participate in the creation of internal controls.

Accordingly, it is highly recommended that internal control system custodians encourage internal auditors to participate in the process of evaluating and designing internal controls. In fact, some entities require that newly designed internal controls be submitted to audit staff specialists for comment and approval before those controls are implemented.

Internal control custodians are charged with comprehensively evaluating the various fraud risks that threaten their employers and assessing what internal controls are needed. In instances where they feel that active fraud-specific internal controls are justified, they proceed to design and install them. In most instances, these active fraud-specific controls are independent of any auditor participation. However, in many instances, financial accounting personnel may well decide that the most effective and cost-beneficial internal controls are focused audits. Once determined—preferably with auditor participation—the specifics of what will be required of the auditors, including the frequency of the examinations, are compulsory and leave no audit discretion to them. It cannot be overemphasized that, in these instances, the primary objective is not to detect fraud. Rather, periodic audits are meant to inject an element of risk into perpetrating fraud in the areas targeted. If fraud is detected, then that is a bonus. But the measure of the efficacy of these fraud-specific internal control audits should never involve whether or not actual fraud is detected.

Remember what was discussed in Chapter 11—people will steal for need or greed and will steal if they believe they will not get caught. Putting controls in place, testing the controls, and letting people know about the process is prevention itself.

Perhaps the simplest and most effective fraud-specific internal control that can be employed is the actual visible presence of the auditor. Some auditors call this practice "showing the flag." The practice involves locating an audit examination in an area that has not seen an auditor for a period of time, in such a manner that would-be perpetrators will be sure to notice. Many fraud perpetrators will be deterred by the auditor's presence. Although some auditors are very discerning in selecting these audit areas, others merely rotate audits in order to cover all operational areas on a regular basis. The interesting thing about these fraud-specific reviews is that auditors need not be doing anything truly productive in terms of detecting fraud. Their mere presence in a certain area warns a would-be perpetrator that his or her perpetration is not without risk.

> *It is easy to follow, but it is uninteresting to do easy things. We find out about ourselves only when we take risks, when we challenge and question.*[1]

NOTE

1. Magdalena Abakanowicz, Polish sculptor, 1930– ; http://www.wisdom quotes.com/002563.html.

Appendix A

ANATOMY OF
A CORPORATE FRAUD

White collar crime costs North American business more than $660 billion annually, or roughly 6 percent of the Gross National Product, as was recently reported in the *2004 Report to the Nation on Occupational Fraud and Abuse*[1] authored by the Association of Certified Fraud Examiners (CFE). Occupational fraud can be defined as "the use of one's occupation for personal enrichment through the deliberate misuse or misapplication of the employing organizations' services or assets," according to the CFE report. This definition is broad and includes fraud schemes as simple as pilferage of company supplies to complex financial statement frauds. However, the massive fraud schemes of Enron, WorldCom, Tyco, and other high profile companies in the past four years have made the issue of white collar frauds a regular topic on the evening news.

The costs of these frauds have been devastating from both a monetary and human perspective. However, the biggest loss has been a loss of faith in the checks and balances of our accounting, corporate, and financial systems. The public trust in public accounting and big corporations has been shaken to its core. The behavior and performance of the public accountants, board of directors, audit committee, corporate counsel, and of course corporate management, all share some of the blame for this situation. The federal government response to these frauds was to pass the Sarbanes-Oxley legislation into law which significantly changed the financial reporting requirements and responsibilities of public corporations, their outside accountants, and corporate counsel. Public accounting firms and corporations lost the ability to self regulate and instead the government has mandated many new reporting requirements that will prevent fraud and protect the public's interest.

Complex white collar scams are often difficult for the media to understand and even more challenging to boil down to the brief reports that predominate in the broadcast and print media. The millions of dollars that executives embezzled in the high profile frauds were shockingly appalling to the public. But when billions of dollars are lost each year from petty theft of company equipment to elaborate financial statement frauds, the time has come for the public to realize how much white collar crime actually costs society in higher prices for goods and services. In cases of financial statement frauds, the real victims, aside from those in the company, are the shareholding public who has lost millions or billions of dollars in market value in the stock of the defrauded company.

Who commits these financial crimes and how do they do it? Sadly, as the following case history illustrates (the names have been changed to protect client confidentiality, but all other facts are true and based on an actual case), the typical perpetrator of fraud is a trusted, educated, longtime employee. This case involves a misappropriation of assets, the most common type of fraud perpetrated.

CASE A.1   Employee Background

Joanne Spencer worked at Fabulous Furniture for eight years. She'd started when it was struggling to survive and had lived through the lean years before the company began to prosper.

Trusted and respected, Spencer was the corporate accountant, bookkeeper, and office manager rolled into one. She made $57,000 a year, supervised several people, and reported directly to the owner. Her duties included paying vendors, depositing receipts, and reconciling bank accounts for the company of more than 180 employees. The company had one owner who made all the key decisions in the company. A regional CPA firm provided basic financial statement compilation and tax services.

Spencer was a divorced single mother of two girls in their mid-20s, one still in college. Her house was modest but impeccably decorated, recently adding a pool in the year before the fraud discovery. She always drove a newer model expensive car, and her clothes were trendy and fashionable. When a group of employees went out for a meal or drinks, Spencer always picked up the tab.

The Theft

Spencer's downfall began during another expensive European vacation. When she went on vacation, she was very careful to prepay bills, take care of petty cash requirements, and in short, eliminate the need for anyone to be in her office while she was gone.

While Spencer was absent, a fill-in employee, who needed petty cash, noticed something unusual while reimbursing the petty cash account. She realized that Spencer was writing large reimbursement checks from the company to the petty cash account each week that far exceeded supporting expense receipts. She notified Fabulous' owner, who in turn informed his accountant, who commenced an inquiry which turned into an investigation.

When Spencer returned from vacation, the company's owner confronted her with the petty cash discrepancies. At first Spencer denied any wrongdoing, but when the owner offered not to press charges in return for a full confession and documentation of how much she had stolen, Spencer quickly relented. She admitted taking approximately $5,000 over a one-year period; however, this was only the tip of the iceberg.

Emotions were running high in the company over employees' disbelief that Joanne Spencer, a dear friend and colleague, could ever steal from the company. People in the company at all levels were experiencing, to one degree or another, the four mental states triggered by fraud detection: denial, then anger, resentment, and finally, acceptance.

At first they couldn't believe Spencer would steal, and they felt her betrayal personally. As anger set in, there was a strong sense she had to be punished, the quicker the better. Often, when feelings boil up, premature and damaging actions can result, such as the leveling of accusations that cannot be proved.

Fabulous was insured for employee dishonesty. To help quantify the loss and prepare a proof of loss for the insurer, the company retained forensic accountants. By engaging outside expertise, Fabulous benefited from an objective approach, which ensured that proper fraud investigation steps were taken.

Even more important, Fabulous learned the complete truth of Spencer's activities, which far exceeded those to which she had admitted. Spencer refused to assist the financial investigators, which raised their suspicions. Through interviews with Fabulous' staff, the investigators learned of Spencer's lavish lifestyle, which included tales of opulent parties, state-of-the-art audio and video equipment, renovations to her house, expensive vacations, and a penchant for expensive new cars.

Clearly, Spencer was living beyond her apparent financial means. This information led the investigators to look into all of her financial transactions at work, other than just petty cash.

Theft Analysis

The investigation revealed that Spencer indeed was stealing money through petty cash. She reused expense receipts, created fictitious receipts, altered receipts, and did not provide an accounting or reconciliation of the system.

The investigation also discovered Spencer was writing company checks for her own personal benefit. As a signatory on the corporate checking accounts, she also had the facsimile signatory stamp of the owner—required for check amounts over $500—in her possession when the forensic accountants performed an inventory of her office. Spencer included her own American Express bill with payment of the corporate account and paid outright many of her personal expenses with company checks.

Each check Spencer signed was painstakingly examined from the operating account to determine if it was used for business or personal purposes. A credit check, which showed that she was heavily in debt, listed many of the credit card companies as payees on the company's operating account.

When the investigation was completed, it was apparent that Spencer had been paying personal expenses with company funds and stole cash outright from the petty cash account. These findings were then corroborated with statements from the credit card companies (and other vendors) in order to file a proof-of-loss with the insurance company and for possible criminal prosecution. According to the forensic accountant's investigation, Spencer took approximately $500,000 from the company over seven years. She originally admitted to stealing only 1 percent of this amount ($5,000) when she was caught.

Although other areas were examined for fraud, such as payroll, vendor invoice files, computer records, and purchasing, it was determined that the bulk of Spencer's theft occurred in the company's petty cash system and operating account. Her theft in these areas was easy because there were no internal controls and no one reviewing her work.

Spencer may have committed other frauds within the company, but the investigation was discontinued at this point because insurance coverage limitations had been exceeded. Fabulous decided against incurring additional costs just to document more fraud, although the company considered recovering the excess loss against Spencer personally. An asset search determined she had insufficient assets for a civil recovery suit. A proof-of-loss was submitted to both the insurance company and police (at the company's direction) to help prove the pending criminal charges against Spencer. The investigation and resulting report produced a winning situation for both Fabulous and the police, although the loss of Spencer as a trusted employee rocked company morale. Fabulous recovered several hundred thousand dollars from the insurance company and was able to write a portion of the loss off on its tax return. Spencer was prosecuted, entered a guilty plea, and was sentenced to 18 months in jail. The police were handed court-ready documents to prove their case, which they didn't have the manpower or time to investigate.

FRAUD PREVENTION TECHNIQUES

The following recommendations can limit exposure to white collar crime within a company.

Internal Controls

Segregation of duties among people and departments is a primary internal control. Many smaller companies, however, cannot afford to hire additional people or have difficulty splitting responsibilities. In these instances, key management/owners can be used as substitutes. Sales and shipping, receipts of cash and bank deposits, and check writing and bank reconciliations are all important duties that require segregation. Spencer was able to perpetrate her crimes for so long because there were no internal controls over her areas of responsibility. She wrote the checks, recorded the checks in the ledger, and reconciled the checkbook. She even had the facsimile stamp of the owner in her office. Because the company was growing and had many vendors, nobody noticed the additional $50,000 to $100,000 in additional payments Spencer made to herself each year through her various schemes.

Employee Screening

An ounce of prevention is worth a pound of cure. A basic background check is inexpensive, can highlight potential risks to the company, and can act as an integrity check to representations in the prospect employee's resume (all references, employers, educational degrees and licenses held are verified). During the investigation of Spencer, her resume was reviewed and her former employer was called. This employer informed the investigator that Spencer was asked to leave after certain questionable financial transactions were discovered. The company never further investigated these transactions, choosing to deal with the issue by not dealing with it. As a result, Spencer got the same type of job with Fabulous as with her prior employer. A simple background check would have exposed her dishonesty.

Verification of Work

Instigate a process whereby internal or outside bodies review and monitor employees' and/or departments' activities and records on a regular or ad hoc basis. This control acts as a powerful deterrent to fraud. Even if the outside accounting firm provides only minimal services to the company, they should be contacted about how they can help with internal controls and minimize the risk of fraud.

Create a Written Code of Ethics and Department Policy and Procedures

Written codes and procedures prescribe how employees should behave and perform their departmental tasks. Is it okay to accept gifts from clients? Can old company equipment be taken home? Can expenses be paid without receipts? When should customers' accounts be written off? By providing a detailed policy, the company not only sets a moral tone for employees to follow, but if something goes wrong, it eliminates the "I didn't know" defense.

Management Philosophy

Communication between management and employees regarding fraud should be clear and concise. The consequences of committing fraud should be understood by all. If employees have a real personal problem or financial concerns, management should listen and react. Open communications may reduce the risk of need-motivated fraud, in which employees steal because of financial pressures. A greed-motivated fraud may be deterred by management's strong commitment to terminate and prosecute any wrongdoing by employees.

Insurance Coverage

Obtain employee dishonesty or fidelity insurance coverage. This insurance is relatively inexpensive for large amounts of coverage.

CONCLUSION

The public has become more aware of white collar crimes and occupational frauds in the past few years from all the high profile fraud cases in the media. The 2002 Sarbanes-Oxley act regulates only public companies, but there is some trickle-down effect to private companies. Sarbanes-Oxley is aimed at protecting the public against the massive financial statement frauds committed by public companies. However, the CFE 2004 report found that the majority of all frauds were perpetrated on private, not public, companies with the greatest number of fraud cases involving companies with fewer than 100 employees. These frauds averaged $123,000 in losses. Asset misappropriation, the subject of this case study, accounts for over 90 percent of all occupational frauds compared to financial statement frauds, which account for 8 percent of all frauds. This means that while financial statement frauds can be the most costly in fraud dollars and human cost, asset misappropriation frauds are far more likely to happen to a company.

The higher number of frauds documented in private, small companies are likely the result of a lack of internal controls, failure to segregate duties, and fewer accounting services by an outside accounting firm. These companies can't afford or don't have the personnel for certain services or controls, resulting in an environment more conducive to fraud. However, there are things that any company can do to significantly reduce the chance they will be defrauded, as discussed in the previous sections.

If employees have a low expectation of getting caught, the chance that fraud and other abuses will occur increases. Through strong internal controls (some of which can be suggested by your accountant) and other fraud prevention and detection policies and procedures, a company's profitability is better protected and the chances of fraud being perpetrated is reduced. As was noted earlier in this chapter, an ounce of prevention is worth a pound of cure. While many businesses have traditionally fallen back on insurance coverage if they discover employee theft, in the modern era it is certainly better to invest in prevention up front.

NOTE

1. *2004 Report to the Nation on Occupational Fraud and Abuse*, Association of Certified Fraud Examiners.

Appendix B

SYMPTOMATIC FRAUD INVESTIGATION CASE STUDY

James Jensen, CPA, known as JJ to his friends, is a member of the Alpha proactive fraud-specific investigation team. JJ is experienced in and tends to favor symptomatic fraud examinations. In symptomatic investigations, rather than selecting audit subjects randomly, one relies on adverse symptoms that may have been disclosed in ordinary business operations and pursues them if they are indicia of fraud.

JJ begins his current examination with a matter that he knows has been particularly disturbing to Alpha management. Among its several business pursuits, Alpha acquires and distributes a high-quality line of hand and power tools. Its last three physical inventory counts of its tool inventory have revealed disturbing shortages. For an inventory with a normal value of about $50 million, the physical inventory counts for the last three years—the last of which was completed only recently—have revealed shortages of 4 percent, 6 percent, and 8 percent, respectively.

After the 4 percent shortage was disclosed, Alpha management was understandably concerned but was willing to accept the various rationalizations offered. When the shortage increased to 6 percent a year later, Alpha became convinced that it was experiencing a serious theft problem but was baffled as to how the tools were getting out of the warehouses. All security was reviewed, and merchandise ready to be shipped was double-checked and periodically spot-checked before being loaded by the motor carriers.

Also, internal security was reviewed and strengthened in several ways. Video cameras were installed at entrance and exit points, merchandise shipping controls were strengthened, and warehouse security reevaluated. When the third physical inventory count revealed an 8 percent disparity between the count and the book inventory, Alpha management went ballistic.

JJ decided to examine the inventory shortages to determine if he could detect any indication of fraud. He began by reviewing the procedures for each of the three physical inventory counts and found no significant reason to take exception to them. He reviewed the security measures taken by Alpha subsequent to the initial disclosures of inventory shortages and found them more than adequate. In fact, he believed them to be excessive in that the checking and rechecking of outgoing shipments often delayed the shipments, with the result that the motor carriers were complaining about the long waits, and the measures were very labor intensive and costly. The videotapes he reviewed often showed the dock areas to be crowded with competing incoming and outgoing shipments. However, after a careful review of all new control measures taken, including hours of reviewing the videotapes, he could see no reason for taking exception to the procedures followed. All shipments appeared to be diligently checked and double-checked as required. He reviewed the entire inventory control system, including the processing of incoming orders by the sales department; the preparation of sales/shipping documents; the distribution of the documents to the warehouse authorizing the removal of stock from warehouse inventories; and the accounting department's inventory control section, which was accountable for processing changes in inventory balances and posting sales to accounts receivable. He could find no deviant procedures that might explain the inventory shortages.

Troubled by the crowded shipping docks, JJ went back to the videotapes and watched them for many more hours, hoping to find a lapse in control. He saw nothing. However, while watching the tapes of the shipping docks, he inadvertently inserted a tape of the receiving docks and watched it for an hour or so. What he saw tended to prove a concern that he had with regard to the labor-intensive procedures used to control shipments. So much labor was required for the extra controls being exercised over merchandise being shipped out to customers that dock personnel were being drawn from the receiving dock area to the shipping dock. The result, as clearly evident in the videotapes, was that dock workers were not thoroughly checking incoming receipts. JJ observed several pallets of tools that were off-loaded from trucks that dock workers had given only a cursory review, rather than conscientiously counting the actual quantities that were received.

At this point in JJ's examination, based on the information just provided, what is he likely to do next? What could possibly explain the growing inventory shortages? At this point, readers should envision a scenario of what may be occurring to account for the inventory shortages and design audit procedures to test their theories.

Comments

Usually when physical inventory counts disclose significant discrepancies between book inventories and the actual counts, it is presumed that the inventory has shrunk as the result of one or more factors, the foremost of which is theft. The only question is how the goods were stolen. Was someone adding extra items to outgoing shipments (defective shipment fraud), or were fictitious sales orders being generated? In this case study, Alpha's efforts were directed toward improving control over shipping procedures, security, and fictitious sales orders, but all measures failed to cure the shrinkage. It should be noted that many entities expect and allow for a shrinkage factor where they are warehousing fragile or highly desirable merchandise. Also, most tolerate a predetermined level of shrinkage as being inevitable. One automobile manufacturer, for example, routinely prepositioned a quantity of parts and tools on assembly lines, in excess of the quantities needed for a given day's production of automobiles, to allow for the shrinkage factor. It expected a certain number of parts, accessories, and tools simply to disappear. However, when the shrinkage extends beyond what has been determined to be "tolerable"—the level at which it would not be cost beneficial to stop the shrinkage—the underlying causes must be determined. In Alpha's case, the inventory shrinkage was considered excessive. Something had to be done.

JJ's examination of Alpha's sales and shipping procedures and warehouse and shipping security disclosed no faults. Desperate for a solution, he reviewed everything he had learned to date and reconsidered his troubling observation of the receiving dock procedure. He speculated on the possibility that if inbound shipments were less than the quantities indicated on the bills of lading and receiving documents, and if receiving dock personnel did not catch the shortages, this could account for a disparity between book inventories and physical counts. In other words, if a quantity of 1,000 of Item X was indicated on the receiving documents, and if only 900 actually were received, and if the Alpha person checking the item in did not detect the short receipt, a shortage would appear at the inventory time. That is, the inventory control section would record 1,000 as received, but only 900 would be warehoused. JJ was prone to reject this supposition as unlikely in that it would require repeated fraud on the part of Alpha's suppliers in order to account for an 8 percent inventory shrinkage. Out of options, he decided to pursue it anyway. He began by preparing a flow chart that depicted the procedure for controlling and recording incoming shipments of warehouse merchandise. See Exhibit B.1, which illustrates this flow chart. From the graphic, JJ saw at once how a theft of goods received could go undetected. Study the exhibit to see what he saw.

For his test, JJ selected a number of recent receiving reports retrieved from the warehouse files, noted the storage locations

Exhibit B.1   Document Flow—Receiving Procedure

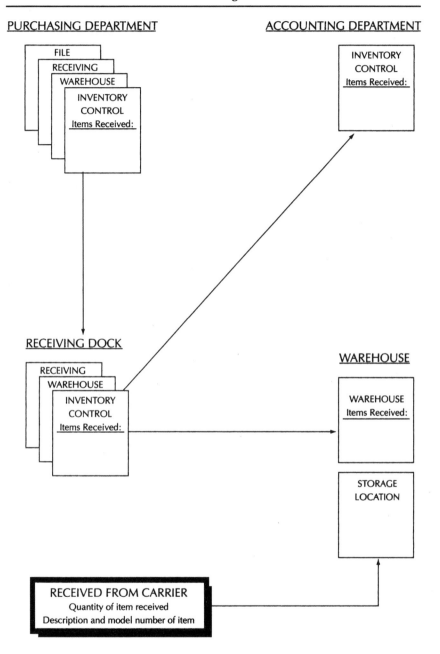

indicated on the receiving reports, and went into the warehouse to verify the quantities. Verification was not a problem. The receiving pallets were still intact, as the warehouse drew stock to be shipped on a FIFO (first in, first out) basis. He was able to trace the specific incoming shipments he was interested in to specific warehouse locations—which were indicated on the receiving reports—to make his counts. He found no exceptions in the counts. However, he discovered that for 5 percent of the receiving reports checked, the receiving dock personnel had indicated that a partial shipment had been received. That is, they discovered that the shipper had delivered fewer items than were expected from the supply source. JJ carefully examined all receiving reports he had selected where Alpha had received less than the complete order. In every case, the shipping source was either highly reputable or the receipts were coming from Alpha's own manufacturing facilities. What interested him most, however, was that all of the partial shipments were delivered by the same freight carrier. When he questioned the warehouse manager about the partial orders, he explained that the practice of making partial shipments was not all that unusual. Sometimes it occurs because two or more trucks are required, or at times when Alpha indicates an urgent need for the items, the shipper may send out available inventory of the items ordered, planning to ship the balance later. When less than the complete order is received, the receiving dock marks the quantity that was actually delivered.

JJ was curious as to how, and possibly if, the partial shipments could somehow explain the inventory shortages disclosed. He tested his theory by inserting into his flow chart of receiving procedures a hypothetical instance where 1,000 items were ordered but only 900 were received. Exhibit B.2 presents his chart. How could this procedure result in the disclosure of a subsequent inventory shortage? JJ was convinced that any shortages were occurring somewhere between the shipper's facilities and the Alpha warehouses. In other words, the freight companies carrying the shipments had to be siphoning off portions of shipments. JJ also

Exhibit B.2   Document Flow—Receiving Report

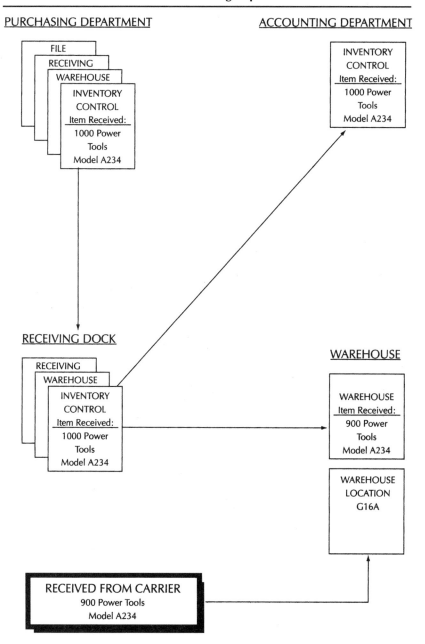

concluded that receiving personnel were very likely involved in a conspiracy to defraud Alpha.

After reviewing Exhibits B.1 and B.2, speculate on why JJ came to these conclusions. Why do you think JJ decided that receiving dock personnel were conspiring in the fraud? After all, they were counting the quantities received correctly, indicating their counts on the receiving reports.

Before discussing his findings and conclusions or revealing his suspicions to the Alpha treasurer, JJ decided to conduct a number of additional tests. Most of JJ's suspicions thus far were speculation. He could not be sure that receiving dock personnel were possible conspirators in fraud until he examined the copies of the receiving reports on partial shipments that had been forwarded to the accounting department. Logically, he reasoned, if the receiving dock personnel were conspirators, they would not notify the accounting department of the partial shipments. Otherwise, accounting would not approve a full payment to the shipper until the balance of the shipment was received. The only way to avoid this was to notify accounting that the full shipment had been received. Exhibit B.2 shows the procedure they would have to follow. That is, they would have to indicate on the warehouse copy of the receiving report that 900 units were being forwarded to storage—so that the warehouse would not detect a discrepancy and indicate to the accounting department that 1,000 units had been received so that accounting would pay the shipper. He now had to prove that.

Proving it was easy for JJ. Using the partial shipment receiving reports he had selected from the warehouse files, he compared them to the copies that had been forwarded to accounting. He found the disparity he expected. Next, he searched the inventory control records to determine if the balance of the partial shipments had ever been received (was it possible that the receiving dock personnel erred in not indicating the partial shipments on the accounting copies?) but they had not been. He was now convinced that there was fraud and that the receiving dock personnel were most likely involved.

JJ met with the treasurer to disclose his findings. The treasurer agreed with JJ's conclusions, was ecstatic that the inventory shortage problem seemed to have been solved, and praised JJ's perceptiveness. He authorized an immediate criminal investigation. A forensic accounting firm was engaged, which confirmed JJ's findings and prepared the case for prosecution. It confirmed that John Doe, a driver for Road Warrior Freight Lines, had conspired with three Alpha receiving dock employees to withhold a portion of selected shipments of goods being delivered. The withheld goods were later sold to various outlets. All conspirators were prosecuted successfully.

Internal Controls

JJ continued his examination of Alpha's internal control procedures and recommended a change in the flow of Alpha's receiving documents. Can you anticipate the change that he recommended?

JJ was concerned that receiving dock personnel could steal incoming goods so easily without the loss being detected for so long. He attributed the problem to the fact that the receiving section controlled the flow of receiving documents to the warehouse and to the accounting department. As illustrated in Exhibit B.2, after they diverted 100 Model A234 power tools, they were able to indicate to the warehouse that only 900 were received, thereby precluding the warehouse from discovering the discrepancy if the shipment was recounted. And they were able to signal to the accounting department that 1,000 had been received, thereby deflecting any likelihood that the discrepancy would be discovered at that point. JJ recommended a simple change in the flow of documents that would ordinarily preclude the undetected theft of goods prior to the time the goods were received at Alpha's warehouses. He recommended that after goods were received and counted by the receiving department, both the warehouse copy and the accounting department's copy of the receiving report be forwarded to the warehouse. The

Exhibit B.3   Document Flow—Receiving Report (Revised)

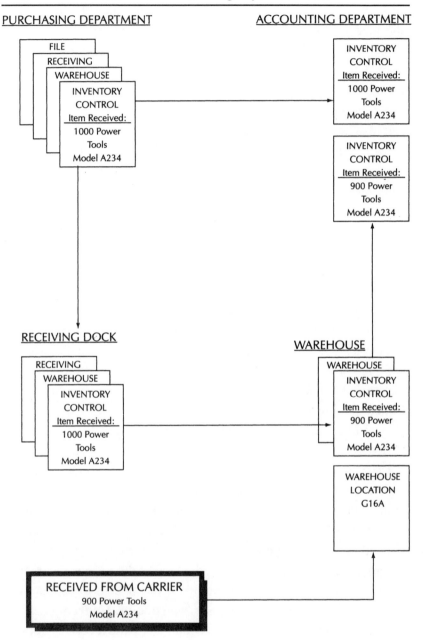

warehouse would be responsible for forwarding accounting's copy to the accounting department. If less than the requested quantity of an item was received, as indicated in Exhibit B.2, the accounting department would be informed of that fact. See Exhibit B.3 for the change in procedure.

JJ had one additional change in mind. Alpha's past desperate attempts to cure the inventory shrinkage problem had resulted in the imposition of costly internal controls that did not produce a favorable benefit in terms of control achieved versus cost of controls and the adverse effect on Alpha's productivity. He recommended that those controls be deactivated.

Appendix C

FRAUD-SPECIFIC CONTRACT REVIEW CASE STUDY

Sandra, the fraud investigator at Alpha, Inc., is reviewing the latest fraud hotline calls, when one attracts her attention. It is a simple anonymous recorded message, received from an obviously distraught female, who insists that Alpha should take a close look at the fire sprinkler contract given to Murphy Brothers Contractors. She states that it involves the warehouse renovation that was recently completed. She adds that she cannot be more specific for fear that the details may reveal her identity, but she sounds very sincere. Without any further hints as to what the reported fraud may entail, Sandra decides to investigate with a wide-scope examination, which she begins on March 13.

Sandra obtains the Murphy Brothers contract. The contract requires Murphy Brothers to "Replace existing sprinkler heads throughout the warehouse area and install new 25-year-life sprinkler heads rated at 165 degrees Fahrenheit: $38,100." Sandra notes that the contract was awarded to Murphy Brothers on January 3. Murphy Brothers was the low bidder in a fierce competition that involved a total of eight bidders. The second lowest bid for the installation of fire sprinklers was $39,900.

Upon investigating further, Sandra learns that 165 degrees is the normal temperature at which fire protection sprinkler heads are calibrated to open, so as to quickly extinguish small fires. She also learns that the renovated warehouse building will be used as an archive to store Alpha computer backup records and a variety of administrative records.

During her examination of the contract, Sandra notes that contract specifications were changed on February 1 to provide for the removal of any 165-degree sprinkler heads that were already installed and to install 268-degree sprinkler heads throughout the new archive. The cost of the change—as estimated by Murphy Brothers—was $40,000. Murphy Brothers claimed that all of the sprinkler heads required by the original contract had been installed, and hence all would have to be removed and scrapped. New 286-degree heads would have to be purchased and installed.

Sandra is skeptical of the justification for this change and seeks independent professional advice. She learns that the use of the higher-temperature sprinkler heads in a records storage facility is appropriate. The use of 286-degree sprinkler heads for archival purposes is a national standard. Experience has shown that where records are being stored, the fire damage resulting from a small fire ranging up to 286 degrees Fahrenheit would be less devastating than the water damage that would result from sprinkler heads activated at 165 degrees

Sandra reviews the receiving report, dated February 21, prepared when Murphy Brothers completed their work. John Green, the Alpha contract manager, signed the report. Sandra then visits the newly renovated warehouse site to inspect the installation. Inspecting the work that had been done is a relatively easy task. No records have yet been moved into the storage area and all the ceiling sprinklers are readily accessible. Sandra obtains the assistance of Robert Clark, and together they find a tall stepladder and begin to inspect the actual sprinkler heads that Murphy Brothers installed. They spend all day Monday inspecting 50 sprinkler heads selected at random throughout the renovated warehouse and make an interesting finding. Thirty of the heads bear the imprint 286°F/2000, the year they were manufactured. Twenty of the sprinkler heads bear the imprint 165°F/1980.

Based on the information provided:

a. Comment on whether Sandra should continue her fraud-specific review of the Murphy Brothers contract.

b. If you think Sandra has not discovered any indicia of fraud, comment on the discoveries she has made and speculate on why you believe they are not indicative of fraud.

c. If you believe Sandra has discovered one or more indicia of fraud, comment on what types of fraud you suspect and why. Feel free to speculate.

d. If you have listed fraud types in part c, suggest what additional work you think Sandra should do to either to validate or to corroborate the indicia you noted, and/or what other action you think she should take.

Comments

The foregoing case study was adapted from an actual much larger and more complicated case. The circumstances described are fictional but are not exaggerated. They are based on actual events.

The first clue that aroused Sandra's suspicion that something was wrong was the contract change order issued on February 1. The contract was originally written to provide for the installation of 165-degree sprinkler heads, which were later discovered not to be appropriate for an archive. Was this merely a costly error, or was it something else? Sandra suspects contract rigging. She asks herself: What if Murphy Brothers Contractors were in collusion with someone like Mr. John Green, and the mistake was intentional?

They would be assured that the contract subsequently would be changed to provide for 286-degree sprinkler heads, which would be correct for an archive. Accordingly, they could bid a low price for the contract—one that would very likely result in a loss—knowing that they could recoup all losses when the contract was changed.

After her inspection of the actual installed sprinkler heads, Sandra is convinced that she has found strong evidence of fraud. Her inspection has disclosed that 30 of the sprinkler heads comply with the contract change order. That is, they were manufactured in 2000 and have the specified fire temperature rating. However, 20 of the sprinkler heads were imprinted with a temperature rating of only 165 degrees and are not in compliance with the contract change order. It is readily apparent that Alpha's John Green, who inspected the Murphy Brother's work, was either negligent or a conspirator in fraud against his employer.

It is Sandra's judgment that Mr. Green is involved in a criminal conspiracy, and she discusses her findings with the Alpha treasurer. She recommends that a criminal investigator be engaged to complete the case. The treasurer is not sure that a criminal investigation is indicated at this stage of her examination and asks Sandra to explain further. She explains that, ordinarily, she too would have doubts. However, her physical inspection of the sprinklers convinced her. She pointed out that 40 percent of the sprinkler heads were not replaced after the change order was issued. Further, she emphasized, the same 40 percent had not been replaced under the provisions of the original contract. All displayed a manufacturing date of 1980 and were near the end of their rated life. Had Murphy Brothers installed all of the 165-degree sprinkler heads required by the original contract, as they claimed to have done, the 40 percent of the heads discovered with 165-degree ratings would have had 1999 or 2000 dates of manufacture imprinted on them, rather than the 1980 dates. Murphy Brothers clearly lied about having installed all the original heads at the time of the contract change order. This strongly suggests the possibility that they were aware that contract specifications would be changed to provide for the 286-degree heads at the time the contract was originally bid. This knowledge would have allowed them to underprice the competition in the initial bidding, in the expectation that they would not have to install the 165-degree heads at all but could claim that they did and claim the maximum costs incidental to the contract change order. The treasurer agreed with Sandra and ordered that a criminal investigation be engaged.

Sandra, however, continued to investigate other circumstances of her findings. For example, she began to look for other associations that involved Mr. Green and the Murphy Brothers. Sandra found that six months prior to the fire sprinkler contract, Mr. Green and the Murphy Brothers firm were involved in what turned out to be a shell fraud. Although the finding involved only a $25,000 job, it nevertheless provided corroborating evidence of a criminal conspiracy between Mr. Green and the Murphy Brothers and an additional example of their underhandedness.

Appendix D

WORLD TOP
CORPORATION
CASE STUDY

Serious fraud is very difficult—if not impossible—to detect in its early stages. This case study attempts to demonstrate this fact. After reviewing it, readers should speculate on the nature of the fraud that may be contemplated. However, readers can do no more than speculate because little or no evidence of fraud is provided—just the possibility of it. Nevertheless, fraud-specific investigators—if they are to be successful in their searches for serious fraud—always must begin by considering the possibilities and specifics of fraud that may be present before they can begin looking for it. Only once the type of fraud is hypothesized—given the facts at hand and regardless of the evidence in support of the hypothesis—can you design your search programs in an attempt to detect it. For the following case study, assuming that investigators entered on the scene in the contract's early stages, their subsequent tactics probably would involve a watchful waiting game to see what contract changes were to occur.

Situation

The World Top Corporation is a leading and highly reputable manufacturer of high-tech satellite launch and tracking systems. It designs, produces, and launches communication and special-purpose satellites. Their products include ground control facilities, antennas, and related equipment to serve a worldwide clientele. The company's primary role is one of conceptual design, engineering, and final assembly of parts and modules that are manufactured by other contractors to World Top specifications.

The World Top satellite launch vehicle is basically composed of an airframe, a propulsion system, and various guidance and control modules, each of which is the responsibility of a separate World Top division. Payloads are also custom designed and built to best serve the needs of each customer.

The high reputation that World Top enjoys is well deserved. Its launches and orbital accuracy are unparalleled in the industry. This reputation, however, is not achieved easily or economically. World Top's improvement of its launch vehicles is a continuing and costly obsession that requires careful management of its acquisition of parts and subassemblies and its evolving designs for launch vehicle components.

Because of the wide diversity of launch vehicle components, World Top finds it advantageous to contract out part and subassembly manufacturing to various specialty contractors, usually restricting its own manufacturing to the fabrication of prototype equipment and final assembly. A substantial number of its manufacturing and inventory responsibilities are passed along to supporting contractors. World Top normally requisitions only enough inventory from its suppliers to meet assembly and launch needs for 30 days. This practice has worked well for World Top in the past and allows the firm to concentrate on engineering, design, final assembly, and successful launches. To ensure launch schedules, while recognizing the production needs of contractors, World Top estimates what its parts and subassembly needs will be for the ensuing 90-day period each month during contract periods. Contractors are advised that World Top will not be obligated to purchase more than 90 days' requirements for any one item.

The contracts with supplying contractors are advertised. The invitations for bids (IFBs) provide interested contractors with the estimated parts and subassemblies to be manufactured during the contract period and their specifications. The contracts are usually written for a one-year period, and low bidders are selected on the basis of the lowest aggregate bid for the World Top estimated requirements for the contract year. The contractors selected are guaranteed minimum revenue under the contracts equal to their total dollar amount bid and are required to supply up to 150 percent in additional parts and subassemblies—if World Top production needs exceed the estimates provided—at the same unit prices bid.

Because of the high degree of technical obsolescence of parts and subassemblies due to the evolving design of launch vehicle and ground control components, World Top reserves the right to modify its technical specifications at any time. The contracts provide that when a contractor's inventory of parts, subassemblies, and related tooling becomes obsolete because of World Top engineering design changes, World Top will purchase any obsolete inventories of in-process and finished goods up to the 90-day inventory level required. Also, the unamortized cost of any tooling that becomes obsolete as a result of World Top engineering changes also will be reimbursed to the contractor.

In a recent advertised award of the airframe manufacturing contract, which included 1,300 line items, four contractors expressed interest in the World Top contracts. The bidders and the total amounts of their bids were:

True Blue Aerospace, Inc.	$12,600,000
The High Company	13,500,000
The Middle Company	11,700,000
Weiss-Kragen-Verbrechen Fabrik (WKV)	11,300,000

Based on its low bid of $11,300,000, WKV was awarded the manufacturing contract. Page 15 of the WKV bid is provided to illustrate the unit cost detail.

Page 15	Item	*	Item No.	Price each
345.	Forward stabilizing control—left	(1)	#135987	$ 231
346.	Forward stabilizing control—right	(1)	#135932	231
347.	Aft stabilizing control–left	(1)	#135322	495
348.	Aft stabilizing control-right	(1)	#135324	495
349.	Gyro control	(1)	#786113	456
350.	Jet thruster-maneuvering	(1)	#994566	11,295
351.	Jet thruster-maneuvering	(1)	#994569	11,295
352.	Jet thruster-maneuvering	(1)	#994570	11,295
353.	Jet thruster-maneuvering	(1)	#994573	11,295
354.	Jet nozzles	(8)	#993436	441
355.	Forward Array Panel	(1)	#456112	3,899
356.	Rear UHF Receiver Bracket	(1)	#511987	855
357.	Rear UHF Receiver Antenna Array	(1)	#115891	13,567

* Quantity required for each launch vehicle.

World Top management was particularly happy with the WKV source for jet thrusters. Last year these thrusters were priced at $12,563, although the higher prices offered on other items dampened their enthusiasm somewhat.

Required

There may be no fraud involved in this case study. Nevertheless, assume that you are about to initiate a proactive fraud-specific investigation of the case. Accordingly, given the circumstances described, speculate on the nature of any fraud that may have occurred or is likely to occur. Adopt the mental attitude of a perpetrating contractor, and consider how you would profit from fraud in these circumstances. You may assume, if it suits your hypothesis, that you have an inside information source. If so, indicate what sort of inside information might serve your criminal purposes.

Additional Information

While the investigator was gathering information in the case at the World Top plant, she overheard a discussion among several engineers who appeared to be excited about a new design for jet thrusters that was expected to maneuver the launch vehicle into precision orbit more reliably. Apparently they were arguing over alternative designs and were unaware they were being overheard. The new design would make obsolete a considerable number of subassemblies, including items #994566, #994569, #994570, and #994573. The auditor knew the engineers worked in a secure area of the World Top plant by the red identification badges that they wore. And, from the nature of their conversation, she concluded that they must have been engaged in designing special tooling for the in-house manufacture of prototype parts and subassemblies. This was consistent with her knowledge of World Top's financial plans, which called for a major in-house production effort scheduled to begin sometime within the next 12 months. She knew the project has the highest World Top priority, and all details of it were strictly classified. However, the engineers had been very careless in discussing their project.

Solution

There are various possibilities for fraud in the World Top illustration. However, the most likely possibility is that unbalanced bidding is involved. Although there is no clear indication that this is so, consider that the price offered for the jet thrusters was considered low by World Top managers and that other items were priced a bit higher than they had hoped for or expected. These two facts alone could cause a skilled fraud-specific investigator to theorize—remember, good fraud investigators must be a bit paranoid—that the WKV Company may have had prior knowledge that the jet thrusters (as well as other items) would soon be technically obsolete and canceled from the production contract. If they were, consider the cost effect. Cancellation of the jet thrusters would eliminate underpriced items from the contract and leave the higher-priced items on the production schedule. Further, in the likely event that the successful manufacturing contractor would also be awarded the production of required replacements for the obsoleted jet thrusters, unit prices claimed and allowed would provide an opportunity for high profits not influenced by competitive bidding.

What led WKV to believe that certain specific parts or subassemblies would be obsoleted by newly designed replacements? Surely the company's speculation had to be based on some intelligence source. Perhaps management also overheard conversations by the engineers. Or, more likely, perhaps there was a conspirator working for World Top who provided WKV with information on the design changes. If so, who could it have been?

At this point, the investigator can do little to advance his or her speculation other than to wait for the inevitable: contract change(s) that would formally notify WKV of the obsolete parts and subassemblies, advising the company to cease production of the identified items and to scrap the in-process and finished inventories. WKV also would be allowed to claim all costs in connection with the scrapped items, up to the contract limitations imposed, and any unamortized special tooling used to produce the items. It this truly were a fraud conspiracy, WKV would be initially planning to minimize its production of obsoleted parts and related tooling but claiming the maximum for scrap allowance purposes.

Once the contract changes are issued, the investigator would have reason to reexamine the circumstances. Fraud would be very difficult to prove, but every attempt should be made to determine the specifics of the crime suspected and who the perpetrators are.

For those readers who may be disappointed in this solution, be advised that fraud investigation is often a most frustrating enterprise. Many times investigators are absolutely certain of the circumstances of a crime and the individuals involved, but are unable to take any appropriate lawful action, which includes any publication of suspicions.

GLOSSARY

accounting, accrual basis: An accounting system based on resources consumed.

accounting, cash basis: An accounting system based on cash consumed.

advertised acquisition: The procurement of property or services based on open competition among bidders.

AICPA: American Institute of Certified Public Accountants.

asset-theft fraud: Fraud that involves loss of something of value. Generally, fraud other than financial statement balance fraud.

auditing, proactive fraud-specific: Examinations that have the sole objective of searching for indicia of fraud before there is reason to suspect fraud.

auditing, reactive: Fraud examinations conducted based on evidence disclosed.

auditing, symptomatic: Examinations inspired by entity operating problems.

auditing, traditional: Examinations that seek to verify reported accounting balances or conditions.

bribe: A bilateral gratuity.

Cohen committee: The Commission on Auditors' Responsibilities (Manuel F. Cohen, chairman), 1978. An independent committee established by the American Institute of Certified Public Accountants to develop conclusions and recommendations regarding the appropriate responsibilities of independent auditors.

collusion: Conspiracy.

committee print: The printed official record of a hearing held by a committee of the U.S. Congress.

conspiracy: The participation of two or more people in the commission of a criminal act, which otherwise would be difficult or impossible by either person acting alone.

contract change order: A formal amendment of contract terms or specifications.

contract rigging: A term used to describe the measures taken by a bidding contractor to assure the award of a contract, with the intention of subsequently profiting through contract changes. Usually involves conspiracy with a trusted employee or officer of the contracting entity.

corroborating evidence: Independent evidence that supplements and strengthens evidence already discovered.

covert: Concealed, secret.

criminal investigator: An individual trained in criminology and paralegal essentials for discovering and documenting the evidence needed to prove fraud. Such investigators often are engaged to react to evidence of fraud detected by auditors.

engineering change order: See *contract change order*. Usually involves product specification changes.

ethical behavior: Conduct in accordance with right or good principles.

evidence: Something that furnishes or tends to furnish proof.

expectation gap: With regard to the detection of fraud, the difference in understanding that exists between what many internal and external users of audit services believe an independent auditor's responsibility is and what the auditors limit it to.

financial statement balance (FSB) fraud: The intentional misstatement of one or more financial statement balances by a reporting entity for the purpose of deceiving one or more external entities as to the reporting entity's net worth, prosperity, or for some other self-serving purpose.

fraud: An intentional perversion of the truth to induce another to part with some valuable thing belonging to him or her.

fraud, defective delivery: The receipt of products or services that are inferior in some manner, without appropriate disclosure or compensation to the recipient.

fraud, defective pricing: Involves charging the victim a price higher than the price that was agreed upon or falsely representing prices so as to deceive the victim.

fraud, defective shipment: Involves the transfer of products or services in excess of those authorized by the delivering entity without appropriate compensation. Invariably involves a con-spiring employee.

fraud, duplicate payment: The intentional issuance of two or more identical checks to the same payee. One is used to pay the creditor, while the other(s) is fraudulent and is recovered and cashed by the perpetrator.

fraud, multiple payee: Involves two or more payments to differ-ent vendors or contractors for the same debt. One of the payees usually is the one that actually delivered the product or services being paid for. The other(s) is fraudulent.

fraud, off-the-books: The theft of assets not recorded in ac-counting records.

fraud, rotation: Fraud where two or more contractors conspire to alternately submit the lowest bid of those that may be in-volved. Normally requires that the contractors dominate an in-dustry in a given region. The practice defeats the theoretical advantages of competitive bidding.

fraud, shell: Involves payments for fictitious projects, materi-als, or services. All underlying documentation is forged. It may or may not involve conspiracy with contractors or suppli-ers. All of the payment money generated is pocketed by the perpetrator(s).

fraud hotline: A mechanism provided for reporting fraud, usu-ally by telephone.

fraud indicia: Hints or clues, usually not evidence, that suggest the possible existence of fraud.

gratuity: Something of value provided by a contractor or vendor to a customer's employee, usually given in expectation of—or in return for—something of value. Note: Although gratuity is commonly defined as a gift, in this instance it is more appropriately defined as compensation.

gratuity, bilateral: Something of value given by a contractor or vendor to a customer's employee in return for specific favors. Always involves a quid pro quo agreement.

gratuity, closed: Applies only to a one-time or specific contract or purchase order. Not an open or continuing order.

gratuity, open: A standing offer of compensation to any customer's employee who complies with the terms of the offer, for example: a new television set in return for a $25,000 order of merchandise.

gratuity, unilateral: A gift provided by one party to another that does not involve a formal quid pro quo agreement. However, the provider of the gift normally expects—and usually receives—favorable treatment from the recipient.

independent auditor: Certified Public Accountant (CPA).

indicative evidence: Indicia of fraud. Something that implies fraud may have occurred but does not by itself constitute proof.

indicia of fraud: See *fraud indicia* and *indicative evidence*.

internal auditor: An auditor (investigator) employed by an entity. Not an independent auditor.

internal controls, fraud-specific: Internal controls having the primary objective of preventing or deterring fraud.

internal controls, passive: See *internal controls, risk*.

internal controls, risk: Controls that seek to defer fraud through certain or increased risk of detection rather than prevention.

invitation for bid (IFB):   A formal request provided to contractors or vendors inviting them to submit price estimates on a proposed contract.

kickback: A share of a contract or purchase order profits returned to a victim's employee in return for conspiratorial assistance.

land flipping: An illegal practice involving the purchase of real estate and subsequent resale of it a number of times between conspiring associates, each time raising the selling price substantially for the purpose of artificially raising the apparent ultimate value.

McKesson Robbins: A corporation involved in a 1937 financial statement balance fraud that reported $19 million of nonexistent inventories and accounts receivable. The case marked the beginning of required generally accepted auditing standards for independent public auditors.

pseudoconspiracy: A situation where one or more people who are key participants in a fraud scheme are innocent of any criminal intent to commit fraud. Their de facto participation usually occurs as a result of their negligence in performing a control function, making fraud by another person(s) possible.

recurring expense: An entity's operating expense of a predictably repeating nature, for example: periodic maintenance.

right-brain orientation: Involves inductive creative thought processes rather than deductive reasoning; thought to occur in the brain's right hemisphere.

SAS: AICPA Statements on Auditing Standards.

SEC: Securities and Exchange Commission.

skimming: The practice of stealing a small portion of a commodity that presumably will not be noticed.

standards of conduct: An employer's interpretation of what is considered ethical behavior.

straw borrowers: Conspirators in mortgage fraud who—for a commission—act as the buyers of mortgaged real estate. After receiving the borrowed funds—which they return to the primary perpetrators—they disappear, defaulting on repayment.

sworn statements: Declarations taken under oath.

unbalanced bidding: Similar to contract rigging. A bidding contractor varies the unit prices bid for contract items in such a manner that he or she submits the lowest aggregate bid, in the expectation that those items for which low unit prices have been offered will be subsequently eliminated from the contract requirements.

world of fraud: All the fraud in existence. The fraud universe.

INDEX

Accidental detection of fraud, 2, 3
Accountants
    ethical standards. *See* Ethics
    forensic accountants, role of,
      16–20
    fraud investigations, 35
    independent CPAs and fraud
      investigations, 34
Accounting codes, 78, 79
American Institute of Certified
    Public Accountants (AICPA)
    Code of Professional Conduct,
      140
    ethical standards, 139–142
    and forensic accounting
      professionals, role of, 16–20
    Joint Ethics Enforcement
      Program (JEEP), 142
    and SAS No. 99, 14
Anonymous tips. *See* Tips and
    hotlines
Association of Certified Fraud
    Examiners (ACFE), 28, 29
    2002 Report to the Nation on
      Occupational Fraud and
      Abuse, 2
    2004 Report to the Nation on
      Occupational Fraud and
      Abuse, 187, 195
Audit and consulting services,
    separation of, 25

Audit committee
    charter, 25
    communication with external
      auditor, 26
    and compliance with Sarbanes-
      Oxley, 24–26
    and initial findings of fraud, 67,
      68
    and internal controls, 28, 29
    meetings, frequency of, 25
    members of, 24
Audit deficiencies, 15, 16
Audit failures, 15, 16
Audit trail, 104
Auditors
    change of, 25
    external. *See* External audits and
      auditors
    independent. *See* Independent
      audits and auditors
    internal. *See* Internal audits and
      auditors
    opinion, 14
    presence of, 185
    responsibilities of, 11, 12
Audits. *See also* External audits
    and auditors; Independent
    audits and auditors; Internal
    audits and auditors
    financial statement audits and
      fraud audits compared, 11–14

229